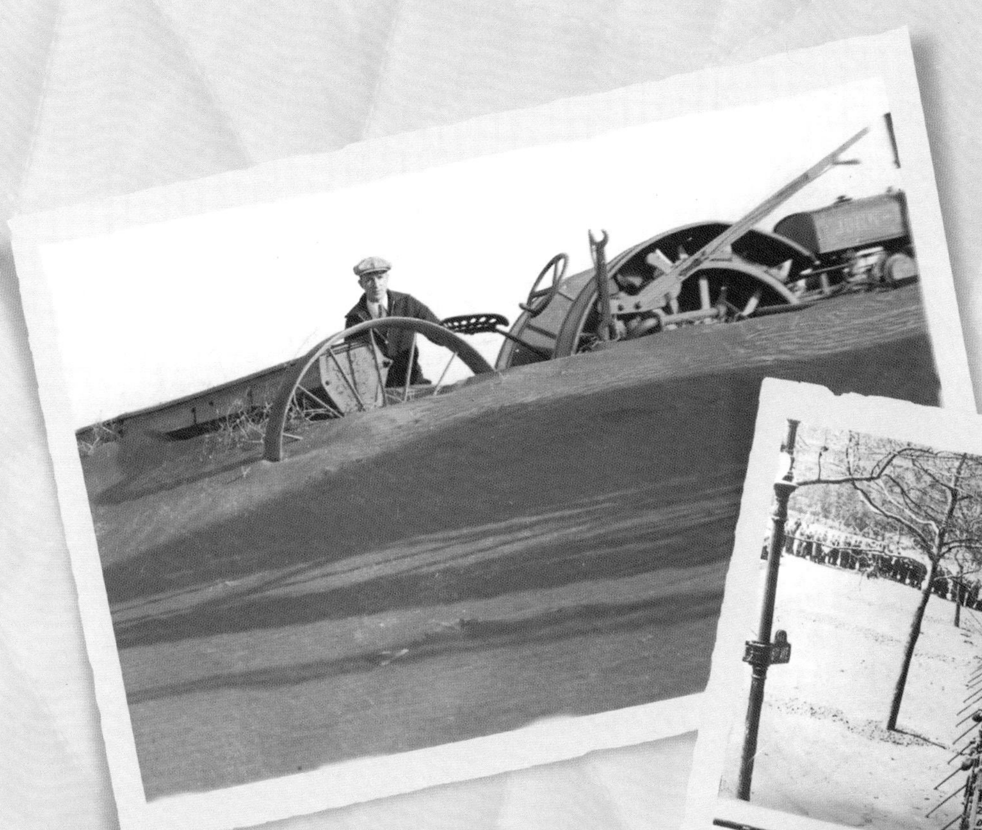

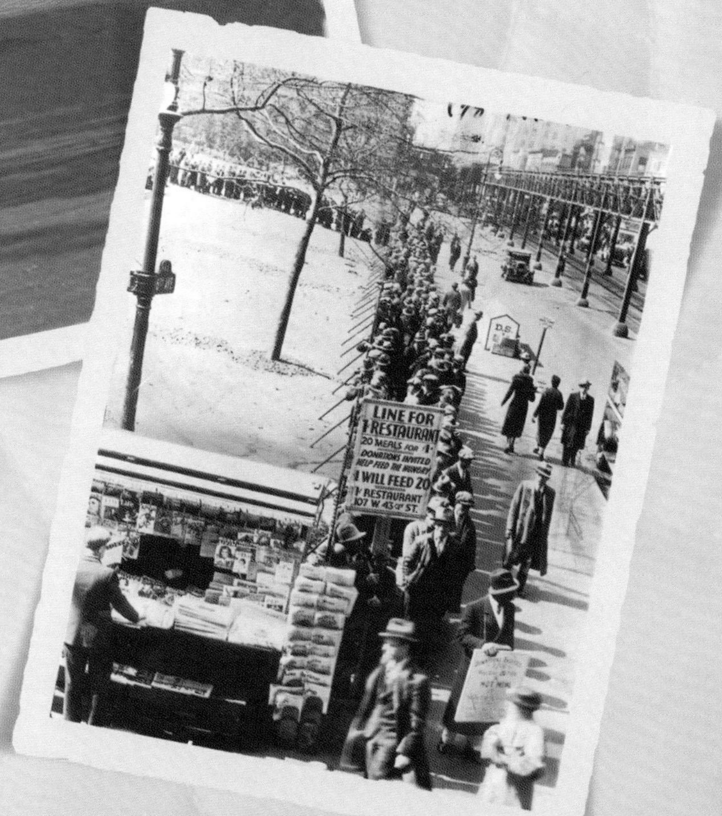
LINE FOR
RESTAURANT
20 MEALS FOR 1
DONATIONS INVITED
HELP FEED THE HUNGRY
WILL FEED 20
RESTAURANT
107 W 43RD ST.

HARD TIMES, *Splendid* QUILTS

A 1930s CELEBRATION:
PAPER PIECING FROM THE KANSAS CITY STAR

By Carolyn Cullinan McCormick

Hard Times, Splendid Quilts
by Carolyn Cullinan McCormick
Editor: Edie McGinnis
Technical Editor: Jane Miller
Book Designer: Amy Robertson
Photography: Aaron Leimkuehler
Technical Illustrations: Eric Craven
Production Assistant: Jo Ann Groves

Published by Kansas City Star Books
1729 Grand Blvd.
Kansas City, Missouri 64108
All rights reserved.
Copyright© 2006
by The Kansas City Star Co.

No part of this book may be reproduced, stored in a retrieval system, or transmitted in any form or by any means electronic, mechanical, photocopying, recording or otherwise, without the prior consent of the publisher. Permission is granted to make copies of the pattern pages only for your own private, personal use.

First edition, first printing
ISBN 10: 1-933466-13-8
ISBN 13: 978-1-933466-13-2

Printed in the
United States of America
by Walsworth Publishing Co.

To order copies, call StarInfo,
(816) 234-4636

www.PickleDish.com

Photos on page i: Left: This is an example of what dust will do. This picture of a tractor imbedded in a drift of dust was taken fifteen miles north of Garden City, Kansas, March 25, 1938. **Right:** People stood in seemingly endless unemployment lines and bread lines throughout the depression years. KANSAS CITY STAR FILE PHOTOS

CONTENTS

Introduction vi
Acknowledgements vii
How To Paper Piece 2

1930s Sampler Quilt
MADE WITH 10" BLOCKS
Supply List 5
New Album 6
Solomon's Temple 9
Chisholm Trail 12
Jackson Star 15
The Kite 18
The Kaleidoscope 21
Feathered Edge Star 24
Ladies Aid Album 28
Grandmother's Favorite 31
The Pine Burr 34
Christmas Tree 37
The Basket 42
Lone Star of Paradise 48
The Broken Branch 51
Indian Trail 56
Railroad Crossing 58
Four Crowns 61
Wood Lily or Indian Head 64
Interlocking Squares 67
Star of Bethlehem 69
Assembling and Finishing 72

Gallery
A GALLERY OF IDEAS 73

Miniature Quilt
MADE WITH 4" BLOCKS
Supply List 77
New Album 78
Four Crowns 80
Pine Burr 82
Star of Bethlehem 84
The Broken Branch 86
Solomon's Temple 88
Feathered Edge Star 90
Ladies Aid Album 92
The Kite 94
Indian Trail 96
Lone Star of Paradise 98
Chisholm Trail 100
Wood Lily or Indian Head 102
Interlocking Squares 104
Railroad Crossing 106
The Basket 108
Grandmother's Favorite 110
The Kaleidoscope 112
Jackson Star 114
Christmas Tree 116
Assembling and Finishing 118

Projects
MADE WITH 10" & 4" BLOCKS
Photo Album 119
Feathered Edge Star Quilt 120
Shadow Box 122

Introduction

It was a time of bank crashes, blinding dust storms, farm foreclosures, unemployment and grinding poverty. Apple vendors were a common sight on the street corners. People who had had money were now standing in breadlines waiting for a handout and wanting nothing more than a hand up. It was a time of eking out and making do.

It was also an era when the one bright spot in a home might be the pastel quilts covering the beds. It

It was a time of eking out and making do. It was also an era when the one bright spot in a home might be the pastel quilts covering the beds.

was splendor in the midst of poverty. It doesn't take much imagination to envision the women of the '30s using every scrap of fabric they could find to piece a quilt to keep their loved ones warm. Tiny little pieces, some stitched together to make the necessary piece large enough, were commonly found in quilts made during the depression years.

Patterns were clipped out of the newspapers and passed from one quilter to another. The newspaper that was foremost in printing patterns was *The Kansas City Star*. The Star was unique in that it printed the entire pattern rather than asking readers to send in their nickel or dime. During the 1930s, *The Star* published more patterns than at any other time during its history.

I first became interested in the patterns and fabrics of the 1930s when a friend gave me a gift of a framed block her mother had hand-pieced decades ago from scraps of green fabric. It was an eight-inch block that connected us across time and space — a simple treasure and a bright spot in my life.

While I was choosing the designs for this book and sewing the quilts, I would think about the women whose work I was echoing so many years later. I wondered about their lives and their families. I wish I knew if they quilted only out of necessity and it was just another chore, or if they cherished the process like I do.

I love the quilts and patterns from this era, and it gave me great pleasure to re-design some of them from that time period into paper-pieced patterns. Anyone can make a beautiful, precise quilt using this technique. You can recreate the depression era look simply by using the wonderful array of reproduction fabrics available or you can use the new fabrics offered by today's fabric designers to update and refresh the designs.

It is my hope that this book will inspire you and help you create a treasure that will be passed from generation to generation.

ACKNOWLEDGEMENTS

They say behind every great man there is a woman. In my case, I have a wonderful husband who is always encouraging and willing to do what is needed to make my life easier, even if that means making dinner.

I appreciate the opportunity that was given to me by Doug Weaver from *The Kansas City Star* to transform more splendid patterns from the past into a technique of the present.

Edie McGinnis, also of *The Kansas City Star*, is a tremendous editor. Thanks for your advice and expertise.

I especially want to thank my daughter-in-law, Megan McCormick, for testing the 10" blocks. I appreciate your hard work.

Friendship is something to treasure and I have the best friends. Diane Donnelly of Bozeman, Montana, thanks for making a quilt for the book. A special thank you to Tracy Peterson Yadon, Lady Quilter, of Manhattan, Montana, you always come through with your terrific quilting. Debbie Dent, Wilshall, Montana, I can always count on you to make a great quilt. Thanks to the wonderful friends who tested the 4" blocks; Marilyn Vap, Ginny Rafferty, Julie Lilly, Jackie Parker, Kathy Safer, Polly Somers, Brenda Williams, Carol Bonetti, Romona Hamline, Carol Neely, Diane Varner, Patrice Heath, and Donna Thalimer.

Thanks also to my wonderful family who took the time to make quilts or help with other projects, Marie Huber, Glendive, Montana, and Tom and Carol Netwal, Castle Rock, Colorado.

Thanks to Amy Robertson for her fabulous design work on this book, to Aaron Leimkuehler, our photographer for the great photos, and to Eric Craven for his excellent technical illustrations. — *Carolyn Cullinan McCormick*

Left: A dust storm bears down on a town in western Kansas in 1935 — that year 40 were recorded in the Dust Bowl states. PHOTO: COURTESY OF THE KANSAS STATE HISTORICAL SOCIETY, TOPEKA, KANSAS
Right: Customers of the Union Trust Bank in Cleveland wait to be paid off following the closing in 1933. PHOTO: KANSAS CITY STAR FILE PHOTO

A NOTE FROM THE AUTHOR

I was born and raised on a ranch in Eastern Montana near Glendive, and currently live in Franktown, Colorado. I have been married to my husband Larry for 30 years. We have a daughter, Jennifer, and a son, Ryan. Ryan recently added his lovely wife, Megan, to our family. The baby of the family is still our dog Jake, who loves being covered up with a quilt.

Quilting has been a big part of my life for over 20 years. I worked and taught a variety of quilting and craft classes at Patchworks in Bozeman, Montana, from 1987 to 1995. In 1995, I invented the Add-A-Quarter ruler to make rotary cutting easier. The Add-A-Quarter ruler has now become a standard tool when using the paper piecing method.

Quilting has taken me down many roads and given me many opportunities. I have met many wonderful and gifted people. The talent I see in the quilting community continues to amaze me. — *Carolyn Cullinan McCormick*

How To Paper Piece

WHY PAPER PIECE?

Paper piecing is great for beginners as well as experienced quilters. One can make a wonderful quilt on their very first try since complicated patterns are broken down into easily managed steps. Sewing the fabric to paper makes matching points relatively easy and the paper stabilizes the fabric, enabling one to use even the smallest of scraps.

HOW TO PAPER PIECE: GET READY...

Use a copy machine to copy your pattern. Make all of your copies from the same original and use the same copy machine. All copy machines distort to some extent so check your pattern by holding the original and the copy together with a light source behind the two sheets of paper. Make as many copies as necessary. It's nice to have a few extras in case you make an error. Use the lightest weight paper you can find. The heavier the paper, the more difficult it is to remove.

Set up your sewing machine. Use a 90/14 size needle and set the stitch length to 18–20 stitches per inch. The larger needle perforates the paper making it easier to tear off. The smaller stitches keep the seams from ripping out when you remove the paper.

Place a piece of muslin or scrap fabric on your ironing board. When you press the pieces, the ink from the copies can transfer onto your ironing board cover.

PAPER PIECING SUPPLIES:
- Add–A–Quarter Ruler — 10" Blocks
- Add–An–Eighth Ruler — 4" Blocks
- Rotary Cutter and Mat
- Rulers for Rotary Cutting
- Sewing Machine
- 90/14 Sewing Machine Needles
- Thread
- Iron and Ironing Board
- Straight Pins (Regular, Silk and/or Flower Head)
- Double–Sided tape (Optional)
- Index Card or Piece of Template Plastic Measuring 3" x 10"
- Tweezers (For removing small pieces of paper)
- Paper for Foundation Piecing (This should be relatively thin)
- Piece of Muslin or Scrap Fabric (For Ironing Board)

Make sure you have a light source nearby. The light on your sewing machine is usually adequate.

Remember when paper piecing, your pattern will be reversed.

GET SET...

Here is a familiar pattern... see **Fig. A.** Instead of templates with seam allowances as many of us are used to seeing, we have lines and numbers. The lines indicate where to sew and the numbers indicate the sequence in which to sew. The only seam allowances that are shown are the ones that go around a block or a unit.

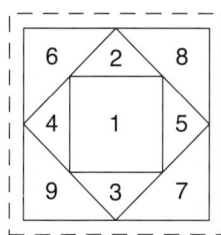

Figure A

The front of the pattern is where the lines and numbers are printed. This is the side you sew on.

The back of the pattern is the side that is blank. This is where your fabric will be placed.

Cut your fabric pieces by following the cutting chart for each block. Always make sure the piece of fabric you are using is at least one-quarter of an inch larger all the way around than shown on the foundation pattern.

SEW!

Put fabric number 1 **right side up** on the blank side of the pattern. You may either pin the piece in place or use double–sided tape to hold the fabric in place. The tape makes the fabric lie flat on the paper. The pin can make a small rise

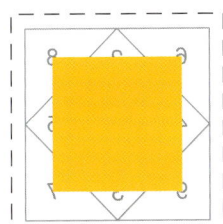

Figure B

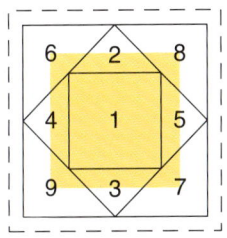

Figure C

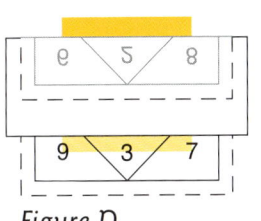

Figure D

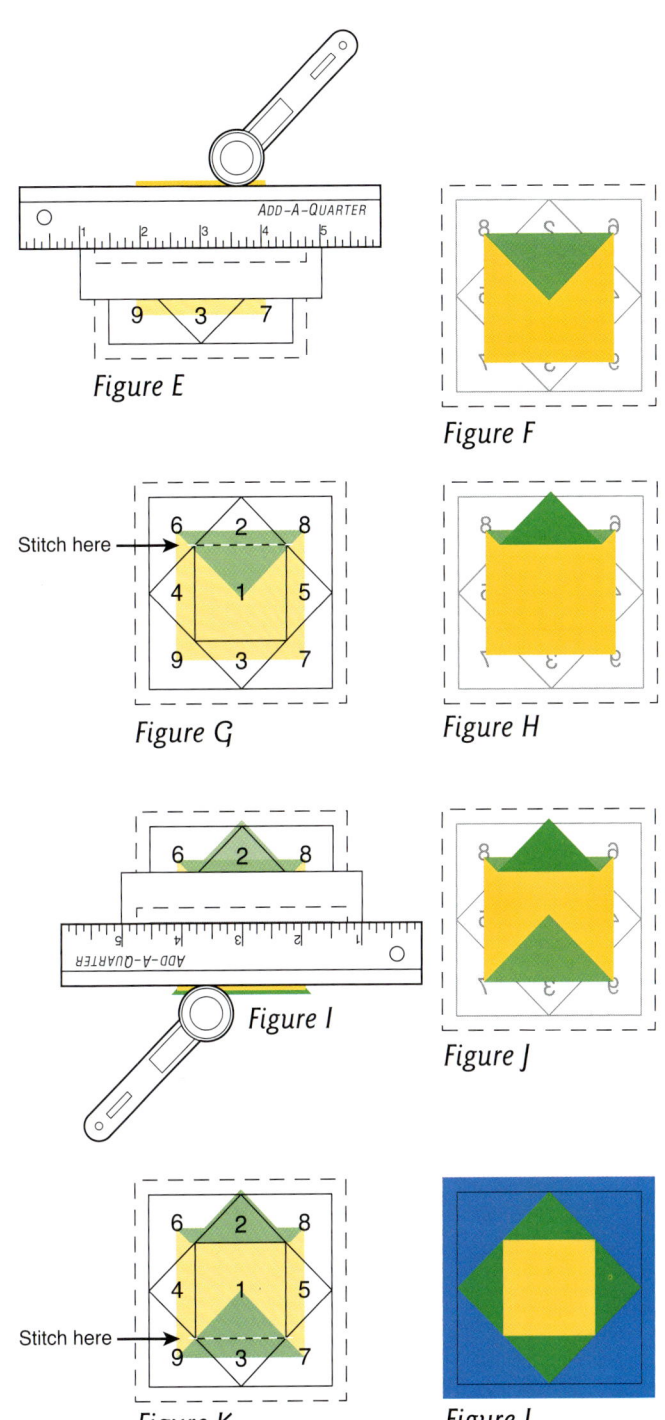

in the paper. **See Fig. B.**

Turn the foundation pattern over, look through the paper towards your light source and make sure the fabric extends over the lines on each side by at least one–quarter of an inch. **See Fig. C.**

Place an index card or template plastic on the sewing line between piece number 1 and piece number 2. Fold back the foundation pattern over the edge of the card. You can now see the excess fabric from piece number 1. **See Fig. D.**

Place the Add–A–Quarter ruler up against the fold of the foundation paper with lip side down. Use the rotary cutter to trim the extra fabric from piece number 1. You will now have a straight line to help you place fabric piece number 2. **See Fig. E.**

Now place the fabric that goes in position number 2 of the pattern on the trimmed edge of piece number 1 with the right sides facing each other. **See Fig. F.**

Turn the foundation paper over and stitch on the line between piece number 1 and piece number 2. Sew a few stitches before the line begins and a few stitches after the line ends. Make sure piece number 2 does not slip. **See Fig. G.**

Flip the paper back over and open piece number 2. Press the piece open using a dry iron. **See Fig. H.**

Fold the foundation paper back along the line between piece number 1 and piece number 3 using the index card or the template plastic. Butt the Add–A–Quarter ruler up against the paper and trim the excess fabric. **See Fig. I.**

Turn the foundation back over and position fabric piece number 3, being careful not to displace your fabric. Sew on the line between number 1 and number 3. **See Fig. J & K.**

Continue sewing each piece in place in the numeric order given until all the pieces are sewn in place and each unit is complete. **See Fig. L.**

After all the pieces are sewn onto the foundation, you will be ready to trim the edges. You will need a ¼" seam allowance around the entire block, no matter the size of the block, when you sew your blocks together. **Never trim on the solid line!** Line up the ruler with the solid line on the foundation. Trim off the excess fabric using your rotary cutter. *Continued on page 4.*

HOW TO PAPER PIECE | 3

How To Paper Piece
CONTINUED

If you are paper piecing a block that is made up of multiple units, the time has come to sew them together. Pin the units together. Make sure the lines you are sewing match on the top and the bottom of the units. This can be accomplished by putting a pin straight through both lines at each intersection. Always check to make sure the seam is directly on the top line and the underneath line as well, otherwise your block will be off.

When the block is finished, **do not remove the paper!** It is best to join the blocks before you remove the paper. This gives you a line to follow when you sew the blocks together. Remove the paper after the blocks are sewn together. You might want to remove the really small pieces with a pair of tweezers.

A FEW VARIATIONS...

Since these patterns from *The Kansas City Star* have been adapted to a paper pieced pattern from traditional blocks, you will have a few things crop up that you might not run into with blocks that were originally designed with paper piecing in mind.

You may have triangles that are either sewn to inside or outside corners of the block. These are shown as separate pieces. You may either pin or use double-sided tape to hold your fabric to the triangles. Sew them in the order indicated on the pattern leaving the paper in place.

Use half-square triangles where you see this symbol:

JUST A FEW SUGGESTIONS...

If you have to unsew and the paper foundation separates on the sewing line, use a piece of clear tape to repair the pattern. Sometimes you will notice the stitches from the previously sewn fabric when you fold back the foundation. If this happens, just pull the foundation away from the fabric and trim using the ruler.

After you have sewn two units together and after pressing, remove the paper from the back side of the seam allowance, this will reduce some of the bulk.

To help speed up your paper piecing, place all of your position 1 pieces on multiple units at the same time. Trim and sew multiple units at the same time.

By placing your pattern face down on a white piece of paper you will be able to see the outline of the design for placement of your first fabric.

1930s Sampler Quilt

GETTING STARTED

1930s SAMPLER QUILT SUPPLY LIST

- **Fabric requirements:**
  ⅓ yard of 21 different 1930s reproduction fabrics
  ⅓ yard of 6 different 1930s solids
- **Background:** 3 yards
- **Sashing:** 1¼ yard
- **Binding:** ½ yard
- **Backing:** 3 yards
- **Batting:** (90 wide) 1½ yards

Hard Times made by Carolyn Cullinan McCormick, Franktown, Colorado, quilted by Tracy Peterson Yadon, Lady Quilter, Manhattan, Montana.

New Album

FEBRUARY 1934 • 10" BLOCK

CUTTING INSTRUCTIONS

FROM THE BACKGROUND FABRIC, CUT:

1 – 4¼" square.

1 – 3" x 12" strip. Cut the strip into 4 – 3" squares. Cut the squares into half-square triangles.

FROM THE MEDIUM FABRIC, CUT:

1 – 4¼" x 17" strip. Cut the strip into 4 – 4¼" squares.

FROM THE DARK FABRIC, CUT:

1 – 5" x 10" strip. Cut the strip into 2 – 5" squares. Cut the squares into half-square triangles.

1 – 3" square. Cut into half-square triangles.

1 – 2½" x 10" strip. Cut the strip into 4 – 2½" squares.

ASSEMBLING THE BLOCK

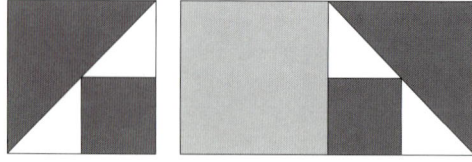

Sew each Unit A to Unit B

Sew Unit AB to Unit C

6 | HARD TIMES, SPLENDID QUILTS

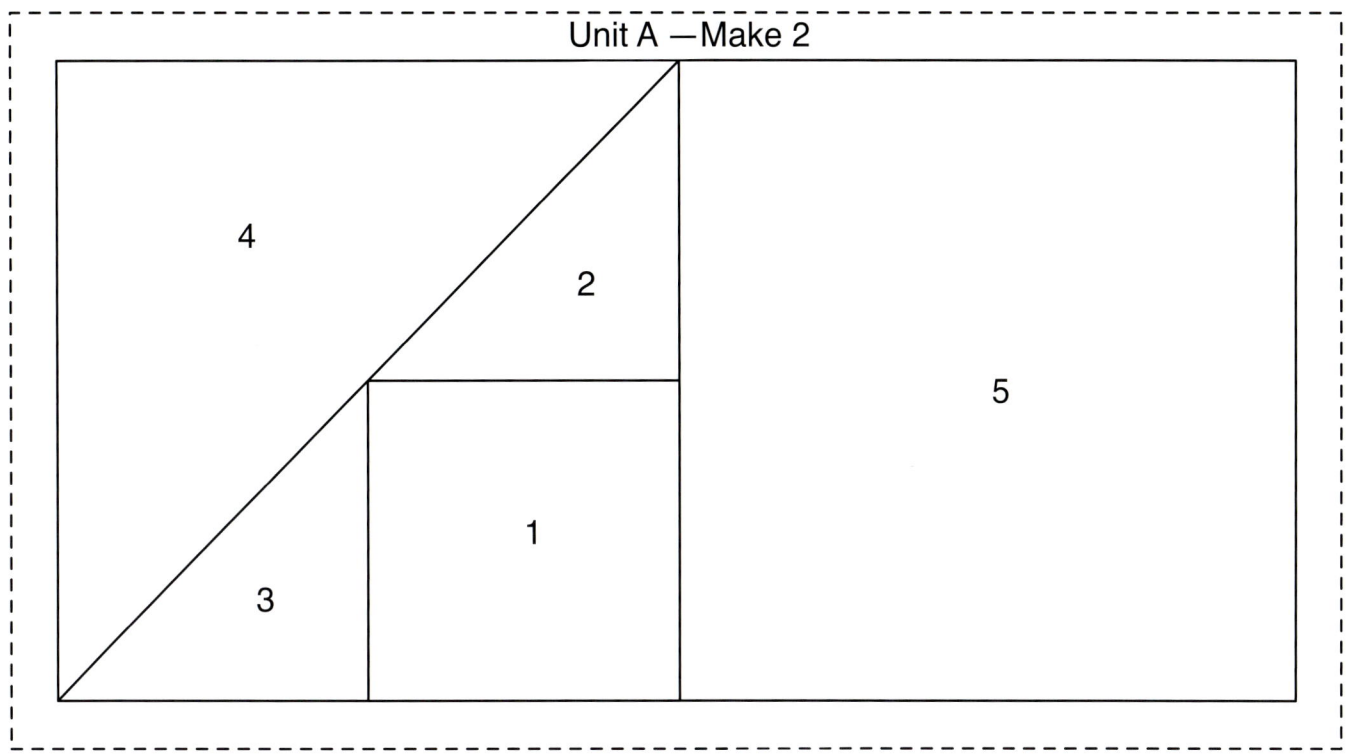
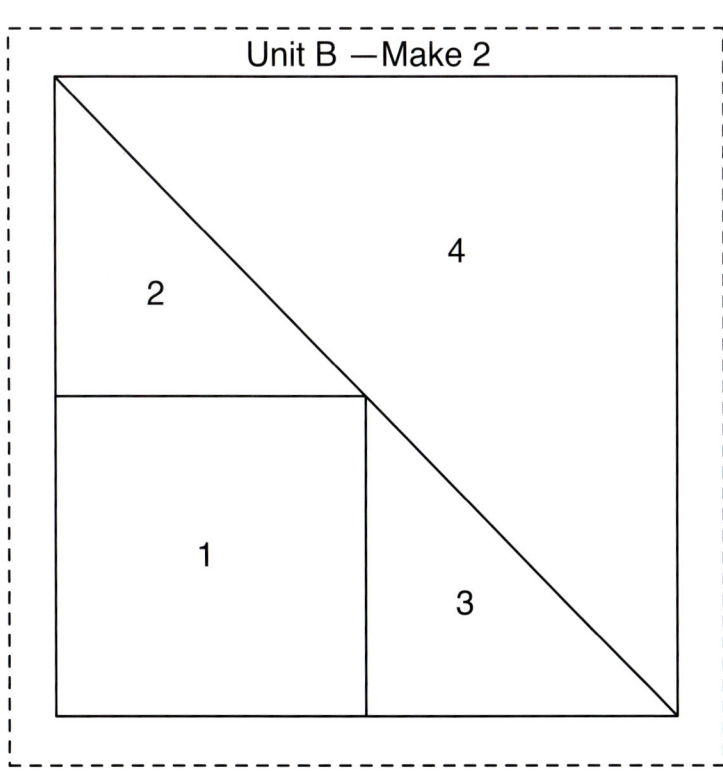

10" NEW ALBUM

POSITION CHART

FABRIC	POSITION	SIZE
Unit A–Make 2		
Dark	1	2½" x 2½"
Background	2, 3	3" x 3"
Dark	4	5" x 5"
Medium	5	4¼" x 4¼"
Unit B–Make 2		
Dark	1	2½" x 2½"
Background	2, 3	3" x 3"
Dark	4	5" x 5"
Unit C–Make 1		
Background	1	4¼" x 4¼"
Dark	2, 3	3" x 3"
Medium	4, 5	4¼" x 4¼"

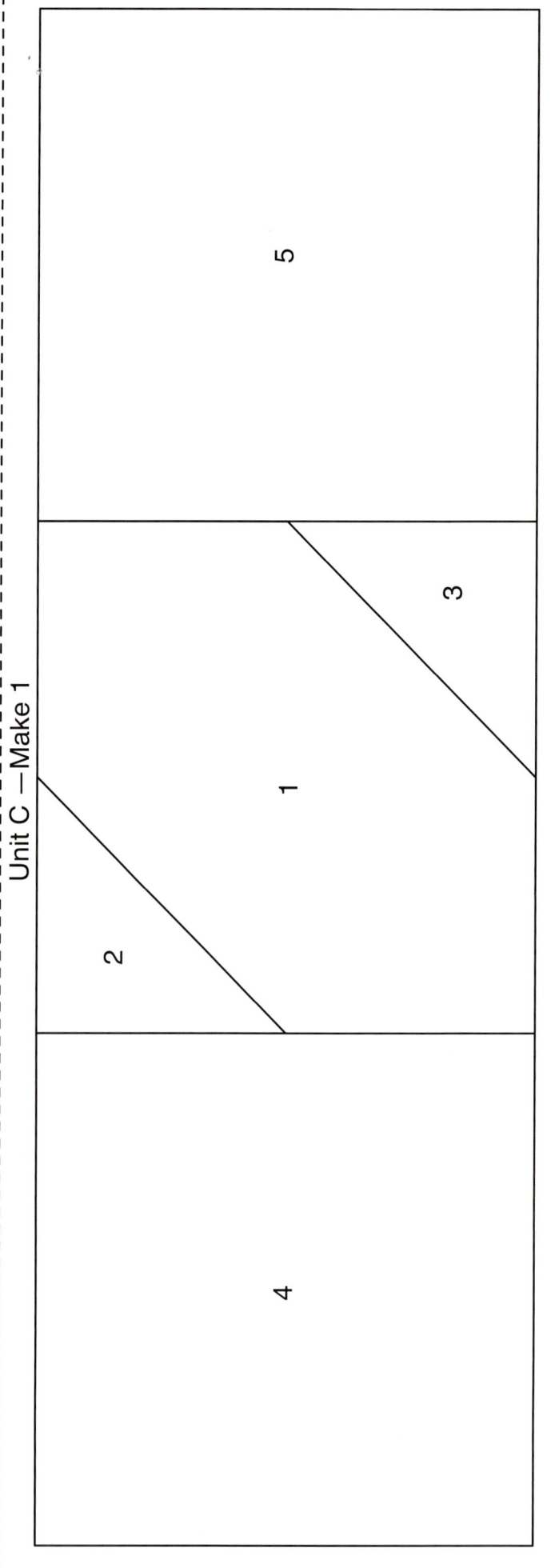

Solomon's Temple

NOVEMBER 1936 • 10" BLOCK

CUTTING INSTRUCTIONS

FROM THE BACKGROUND FABRIC, CUT:

1 – 5¼" x 10½" strip. Cut the strip into 2 – 5¼" squares. Cut the squares into half-square triangles.

1 – 2½" x 40" strip and 1 – 2½" x 5" strip. Cut the strips into 18 – 2½" squares. Cut the squares into half-square triangles.

1 – 2" x 12" strip. Cut the strip into 6 – 2" squares.

FROM THE MEDIUM FABRIC, CUT:

1 – 4¾" x 9½" strip. Cut the strip into 2 – 4¾" squares. Cut the squares into half-square triangles.

1 – 4" square.

1 – 2½" x 40" strip and 1 – 2½" x 15" strip. Cut the strips into 22 – 2½" squares. Cut the squares into half-square triangles.

1 – 2" x 4" strip. Cut the strip into 2 – 2" squares.

ASSEMBLING THE BLOCK

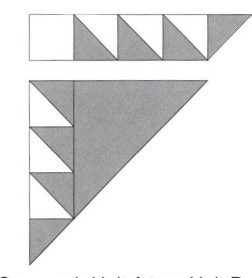

Sew each Unit A to a Unit B

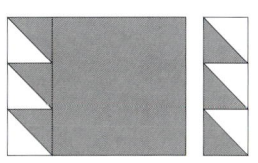

Sew Unit D to Unit E

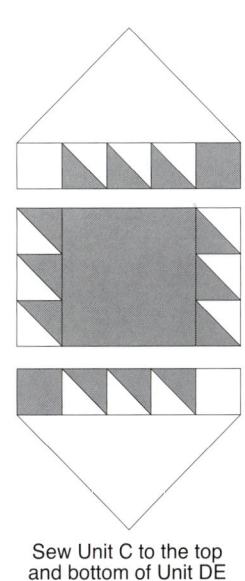

Sew Unit C to the top and bottom of Unit DE

Sew each Unit F to both sides of Unit CDE

Assembling instructions continued on page 10.

ASSEMBLING THE BLOCK

Assembling instructions continued from page 9.

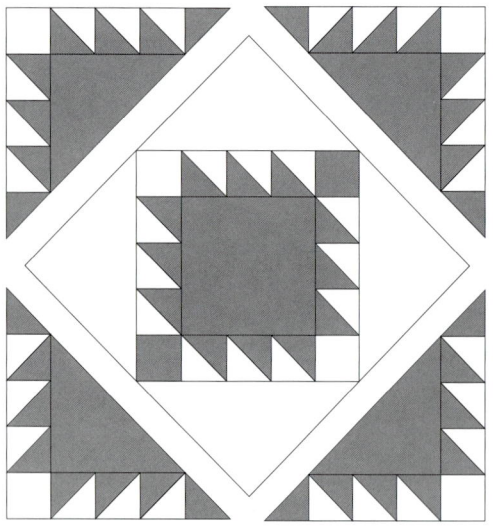

Sew each AB Unit to Unit CDEF

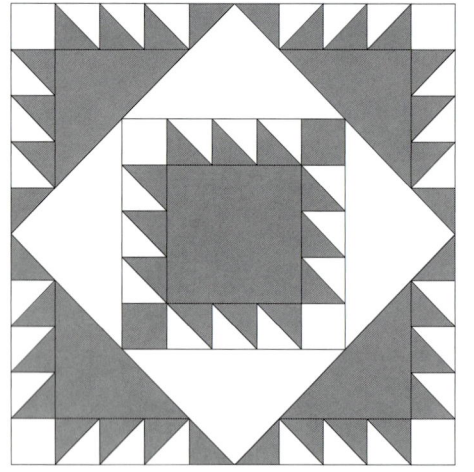

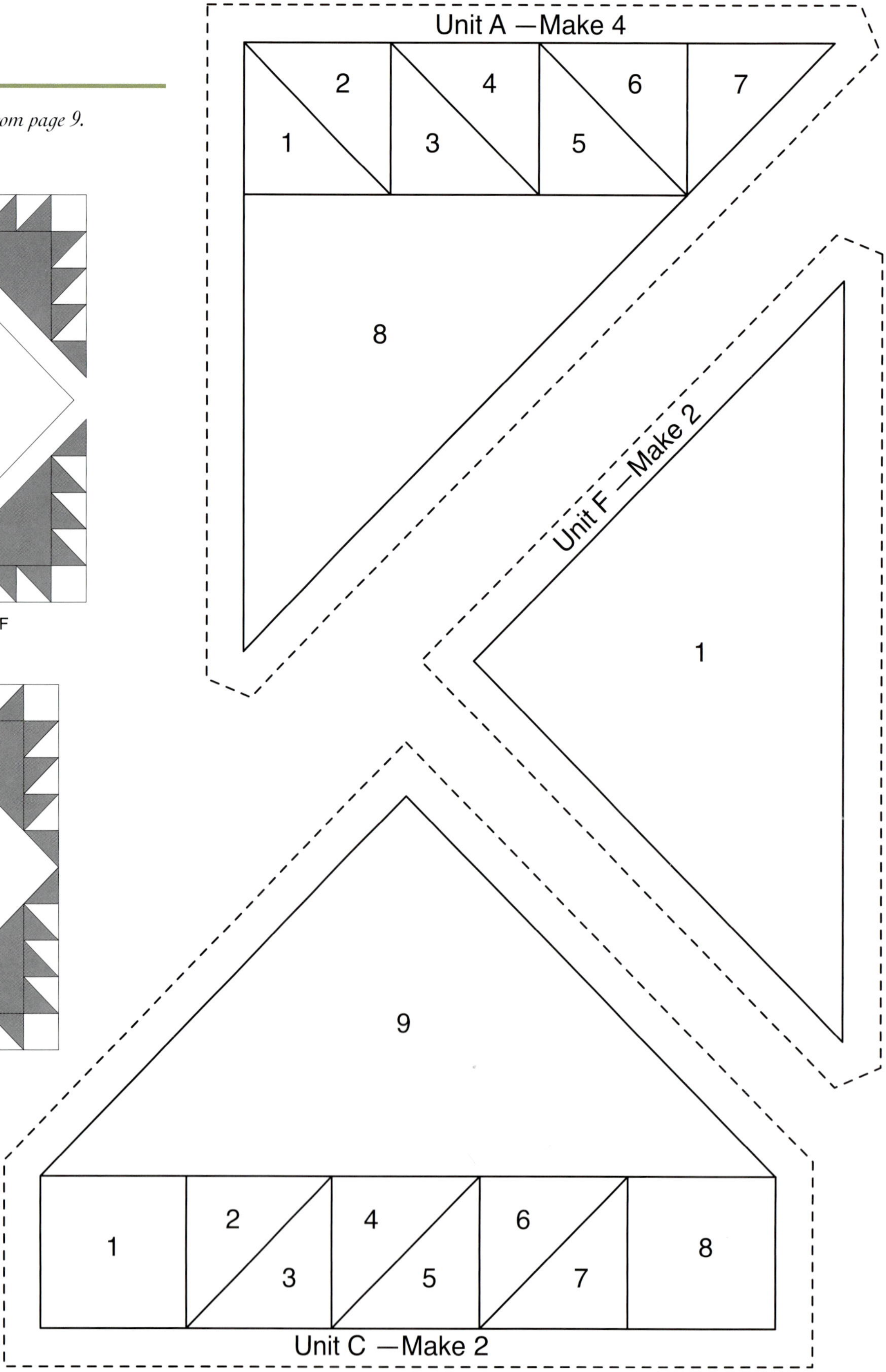
Unit A —Make 4
2
4
6
7
1
3
5
8
Unit F —Make 2
1
9
2
4
6
1
8
3
5
7
Unit C —Make 2

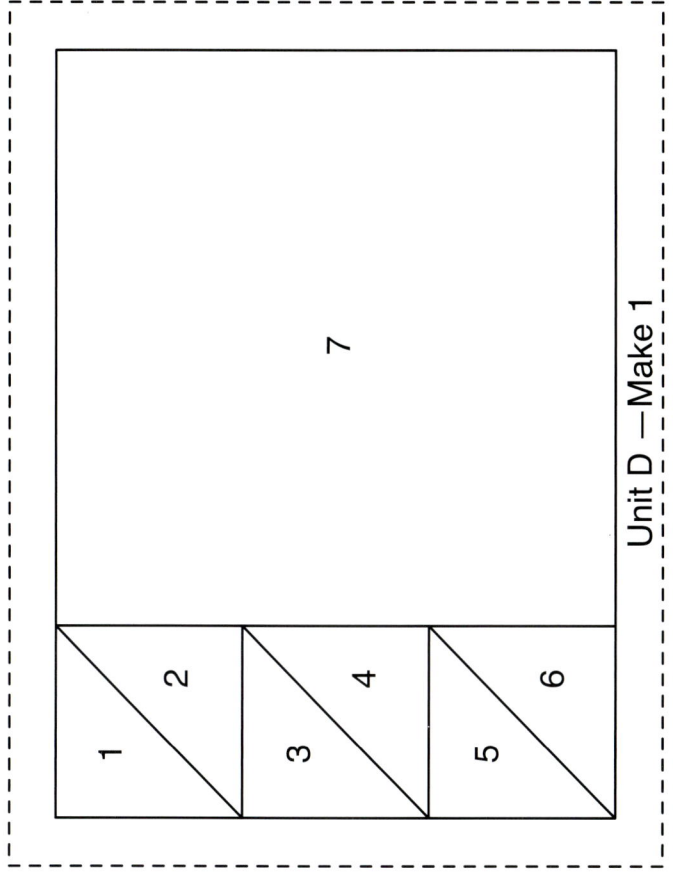

POSITION CHART

FABRIC	POSITION	SIZE
Unit A–Make 4		
Medium	1, 3, 5, 7	2½" x 2½"
Background	2, 4, 6	2½" x 2½"
Medium	8	4¾" x 4¾"
Unit B–Make 4		
Medium	1, 3, 5, 7	2½" x 2½"
Background	2, 4, 6	2½" x 2½"
Background	8	2" x 2"
Unit C–Make 2		
Medium	1	2" x 2"
Background	2, 4, 6	2½" x 2½"
Medium	3, 5, 7	2½" x 2½"
Background	8	2" x 2"
Background	9	5¼" x 5¼"
Unit D–Make 1		
Background	1, 3, 5	2½" x 2½"
Medium	2, 4, 6	2½" x 2½"
Medium	7	4" x 4"
Unit E–Make 1		
Medium	1, 3, 5	2½" x 2½"
Background	2, 4, 6	2½" x 2½"
Unit F–Make 2		
Background	1	5¼" x 5¼"

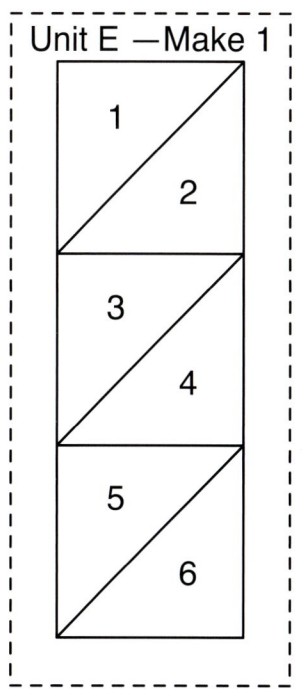

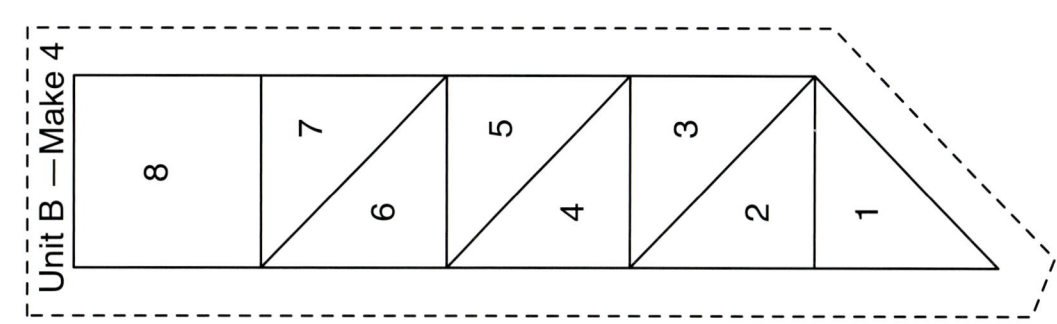

10" SOLOMON'S TEMPLE | 11

Chisholm Trail

MAY 1939 • 10" BLOCK

CUTTING INSTRUCTIONS

FROM THE BACKGROUND FABRIC, CUT:

1 – 5½" square. Cut the square into half-square triangles.

1 – 4¼" x 21¼" strip. Cut the strip into 5 – 4¼" squares. Cut the squares into half-square triangles.

FROM THE MEDIUM FABRIC, CUT:

1 – 4¼" x 29¾" strip. Cut the strip into 7 – 4¼" squares. Cut the squares into half-square triangles.

FROM THE DARK FABRIC, CUT:

1 – 3½" x 7" strip. Cut the strip into 2 – 3½" squares.

ASSEMBLING THE BLOCK

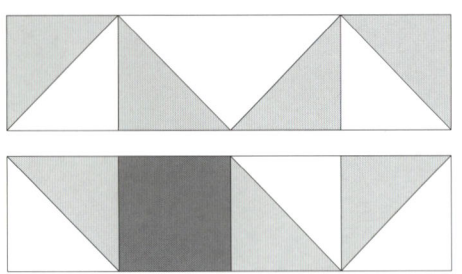

Sew each Unit A to each Unit B

Sew AB units together

12 | HARD TIMES, SPLENDID QUILTS

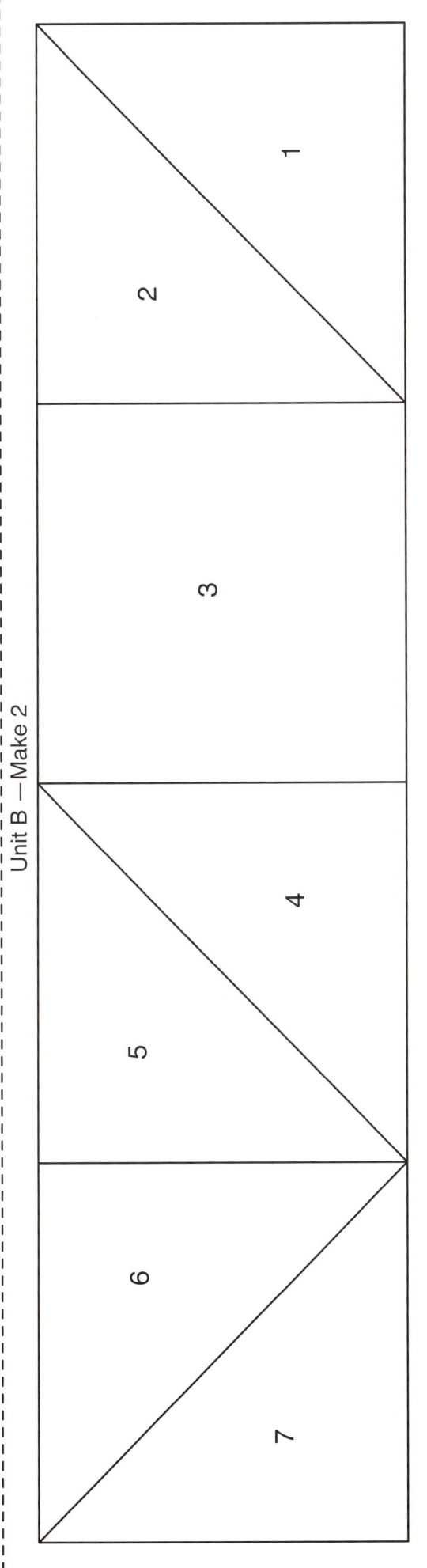

POSITION CHART

FABRIC	POSITION	SIZE
Unit A–Make 2		
Background	1	5½" x 5½"
Medium	2, 3	4¼" x 4¼"
Background	4, 5	4¼" x 4¼"
Medium	6, 7	4¼" x 4¼"
Unit B–Make 2		
Background	1, 5, 7	4¼" x 4¼"
Medium	2, 4, 6	4¼" x 4¼"
Dark	3	3½" x 3½"

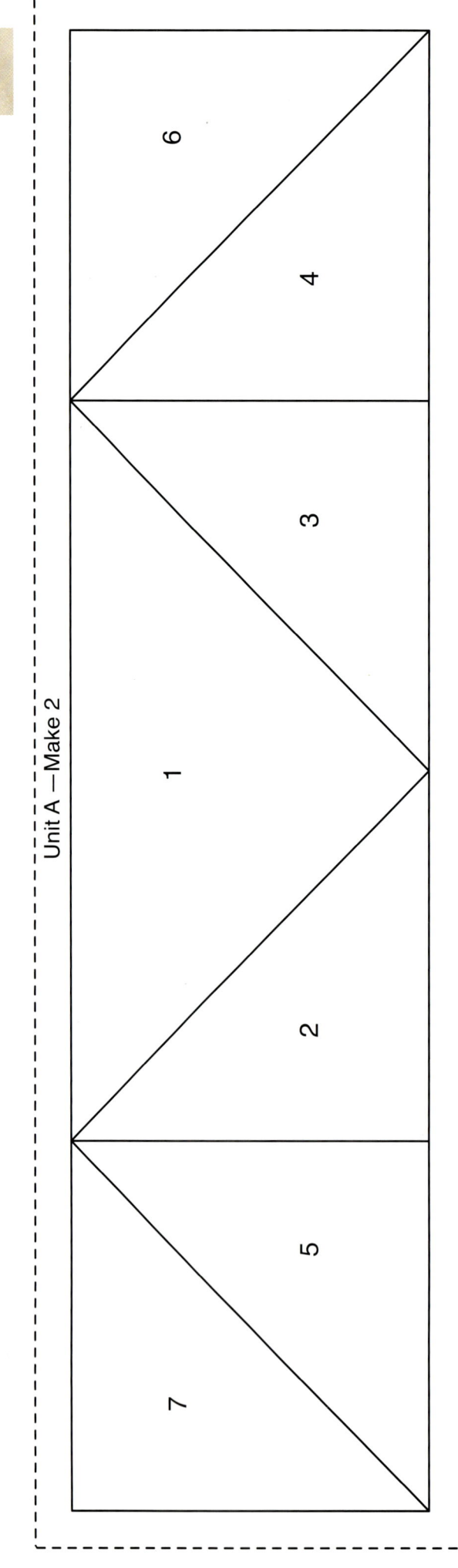

Unit A —Make 2

14 | HARD TIMES, SPLENDID QUILTS

Jackson Star

MAY 1931 • 10" BLOCK

ASSEMBLING THE BLOCK

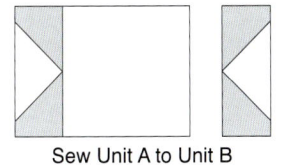

Sew Unit A to Unit B

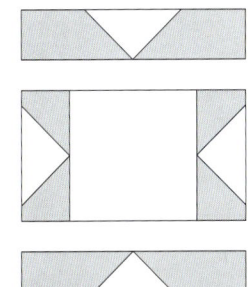

Sew each Unit C to Unit AB

Assembling instructions continued on page 16.

CUTTING INSTRUCTIONS

FROM THE BACKGROUND FABRIC, CUT:

1 – 3¾" square.

1 – 3½" x 7" strip. Cut the strip into 2 – 3½" squares. Cut the squares into half-square triangles.

1 – 3¼" x 39" strip. Cut the strip into 12 – 3¼" squares. Cut the squares into half-square triangles.

1 – 2¼" x 9" strip. Cut the strip into 4 – 2¼" squares.

FROM THE MEDIUM FABRIC, CUT:

1 – 2¾" x 15" strip. Cut the strip into 4 – 2¾" x 3¾" rectangles.

1 – 2" x 11" strip. Cut the strip into 4 – 2" x 2¾" rectangles.

FROM THE DARK FABRIC, CUT:

1 – 3¼" x 13" strip. Cut the strip into 4 – 3¼" squares. Cut the squares into half-square triangles.

1 – 2" x 28" strip. Cut the strip into 8 – 2" x 3½" rectangles.

1 – 1¾" x 24" strip. Cut the strip into 4 – 1¾" x 6" rectangles

POSITION CHART

FABRIC	POSITION	SIZE
Unit A–Make 1		
Background	1	3¼" x 3¼"
Medium	2, 3	2" x 2¾"
Background	4	3¾" x 3¾"
Unit B–Make 1		
Background	1	3¼" x 3¼"
Medium	2, 3	2" x 2¾"
Unit C–Make 2		
Background	1	3¼" x 3¼"
Medium	2, 3	2¾" x 3¾"
Unit D–Make 4		
Background	1	3¼" x 3¼"
Dark	2, 3	2" x 3½"
Background	4	3½" x 3½"
Unit E–Make 4		
Background	1	2¼" x 2¼"
Dark	2, 3	3¼" x 3¼"
Background	4, 5, 7, 8	3¼" x 3¼"
Dark	6	1¾" x 6"

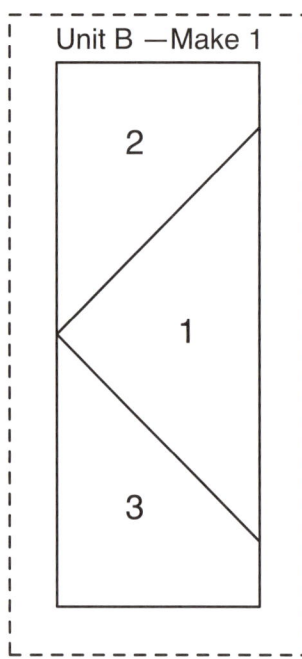

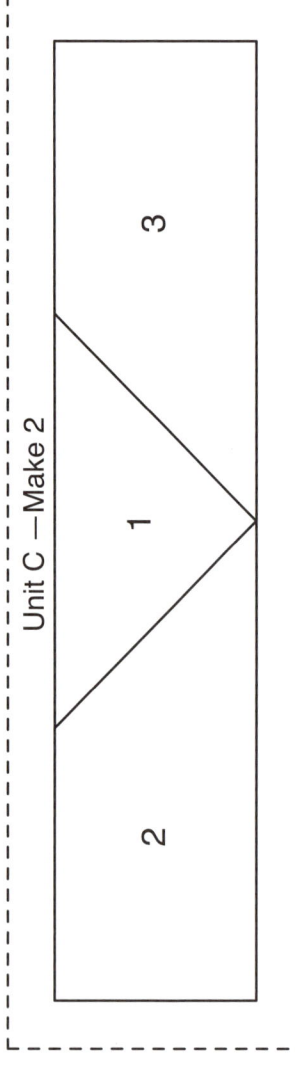

ASSEMBLING THE BLOCK

Assembling instructions continued from page 15.

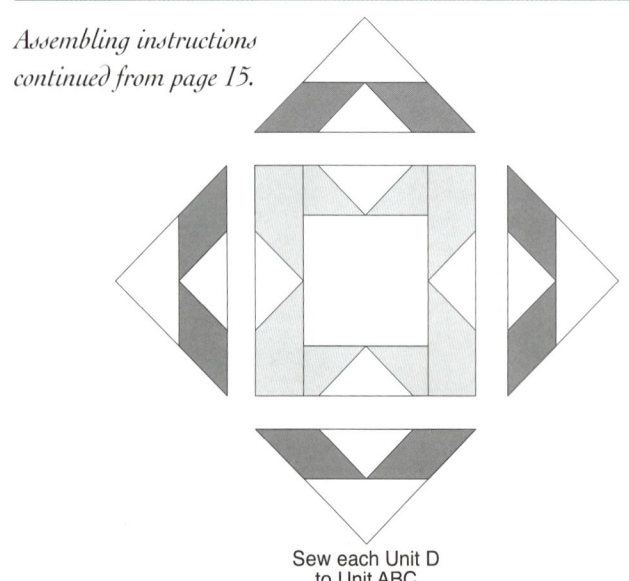

Sew each Unit D to Unit ABC

Sew each Unit E to ABCD

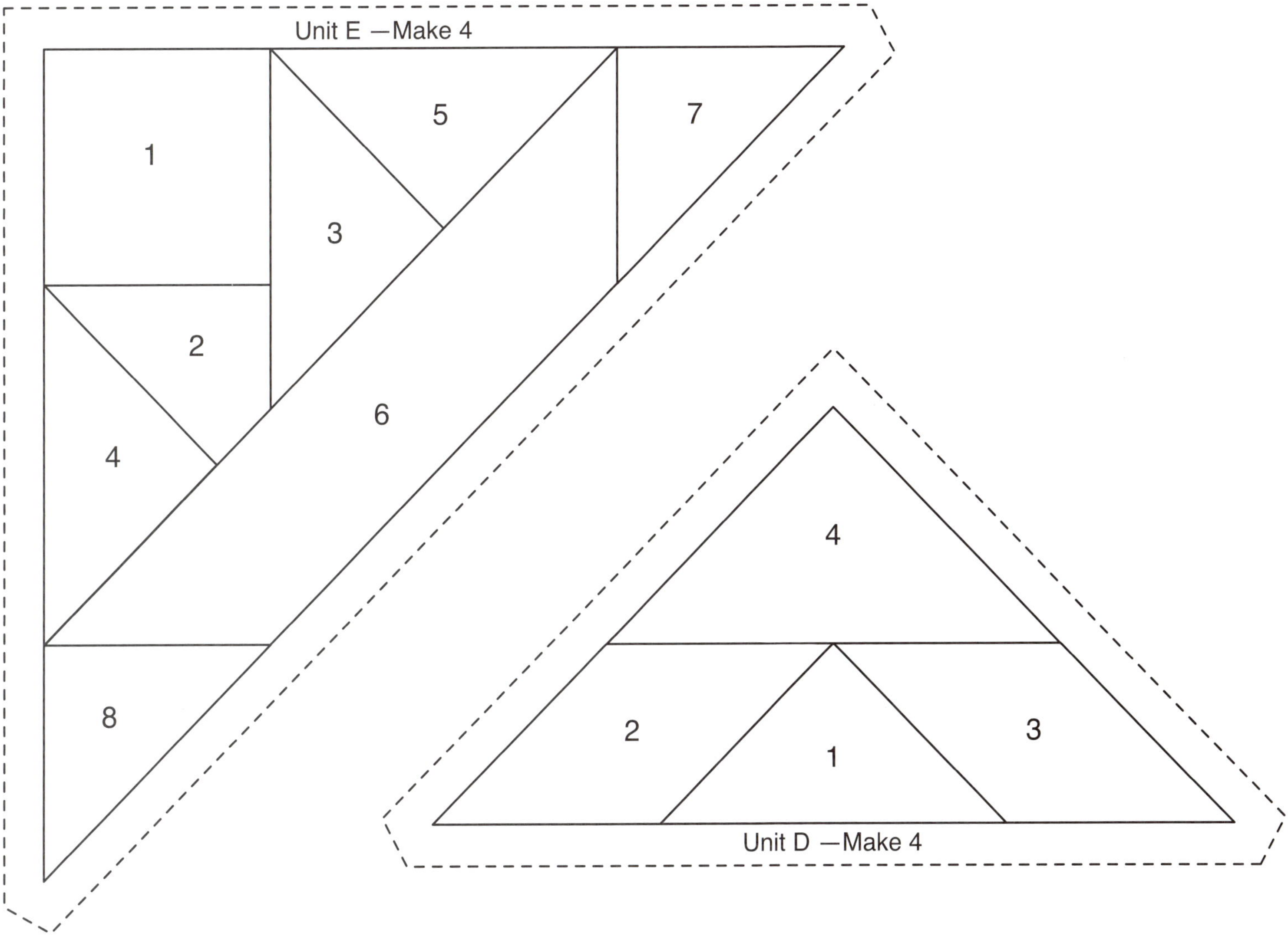

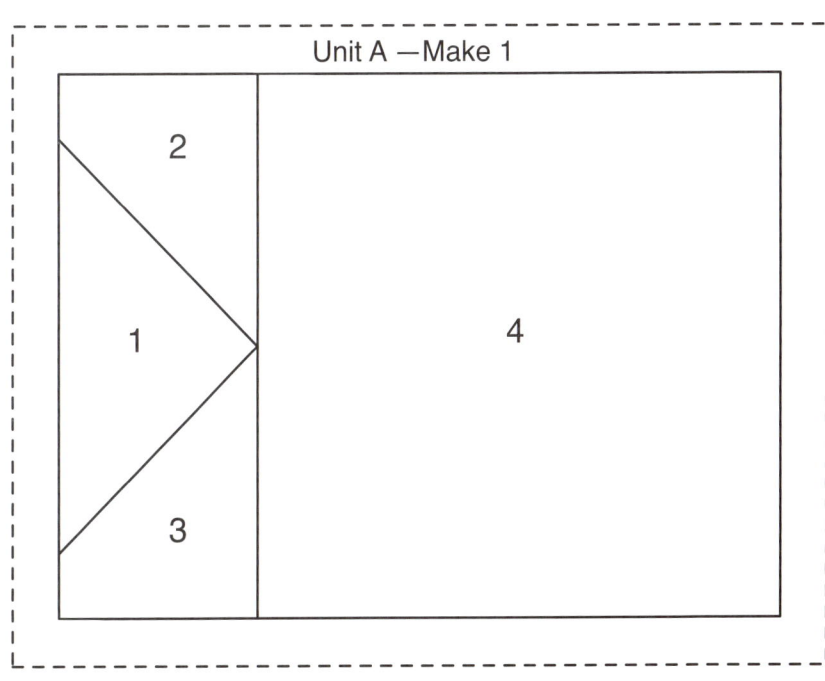

10" JACKSON STAR

The Kite

JANUARY 1937 • 10" BLOCK

CUTTING INSTRUCTIONS

FROM THE BACKGROUND FABRIC, CUT:

1 – 5¼" x 10½" strip. Cut the strip into 2 – 5¼" squares. Cut the squares into half-square triangles.

1 – 2¾" x 11" strip. Cut the strip into 4 – 2¾" squares. Cut the squares into half-square triangles.

1 – 2½" x 26" strip. Cut the strip into 8 – 2½" x 3¼" rectangles.

1 – 2½" x 18" strip. Cut the strip into 4 – 2½" x 4½" rectangles.

FROM THE MEDIUM FABRIC, CUT:

1 – 3¼" x 17" strip. Cut the strip into 4 – 3¼" x 4¼" rectangles.

1 – 1¾" x 36" strip. Cut the strip into 16 – 1¾" x 2¼" rectangles.

FROM THE DARK FABRIC, CUT:

1 – 3" x 22" strip. Cut the strip into 4 – 3" x 5½" rectangles.

ASSEMBLING THE BLOCK

Sew each Unit B to a Unit C

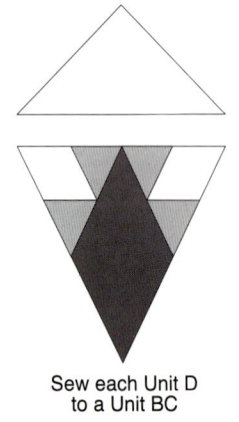

Sew each Unit D to a Unit BC

Sew each Unit A to a Unit BCD

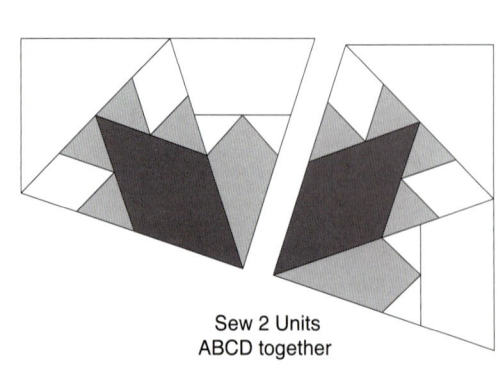

Sew 2 Units ABCD together

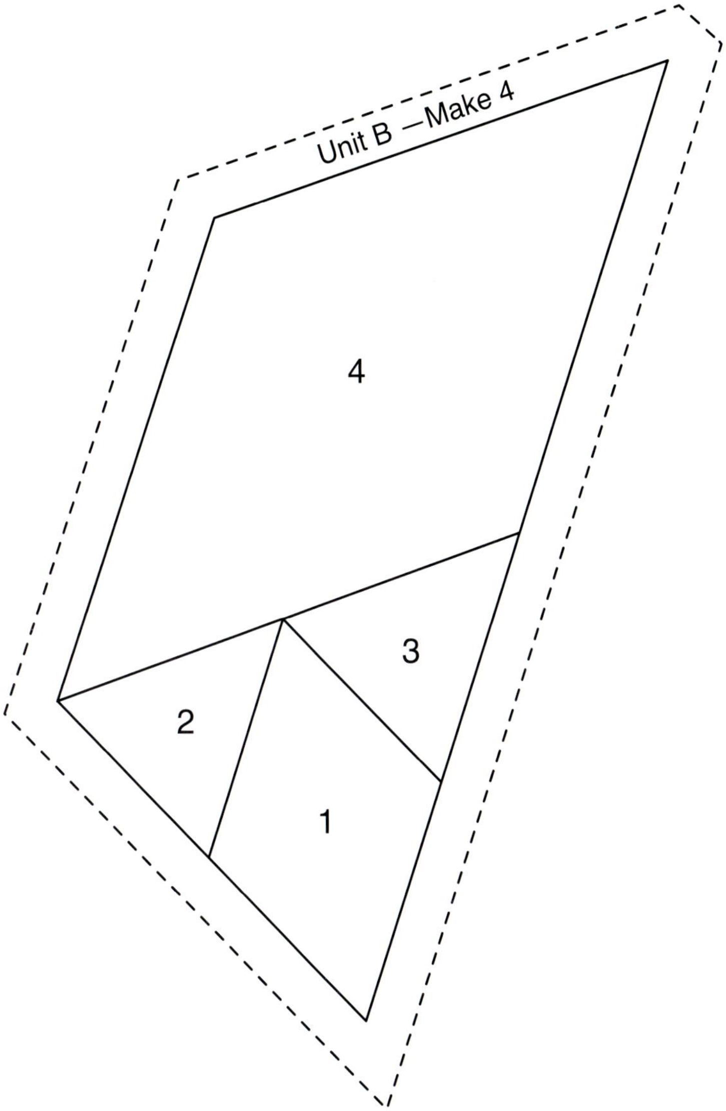

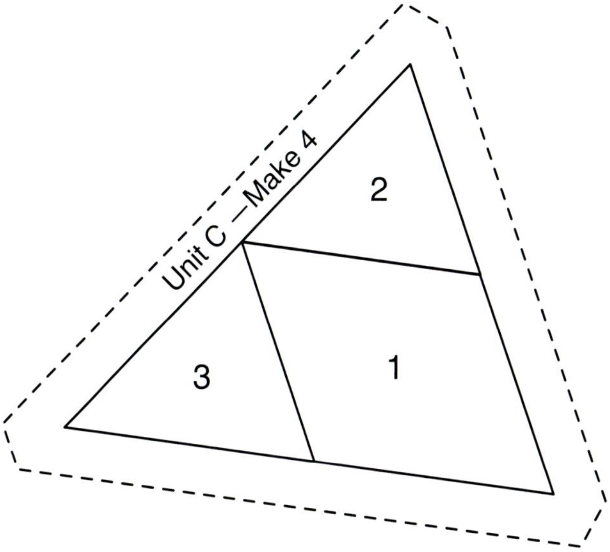

Unit B — Make 4

4
2
3
1

Unit C — Make 4

2
3
1

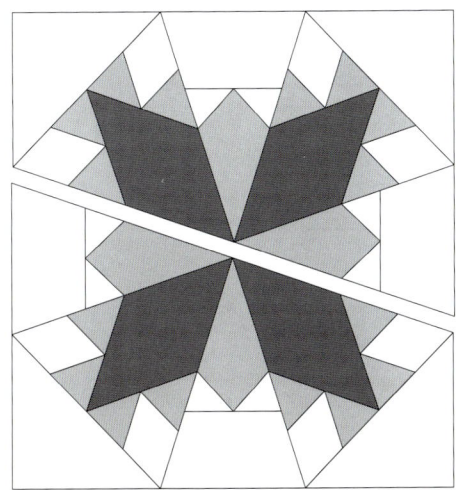

Sew the two halves together to complete the block.

10" THE KITE

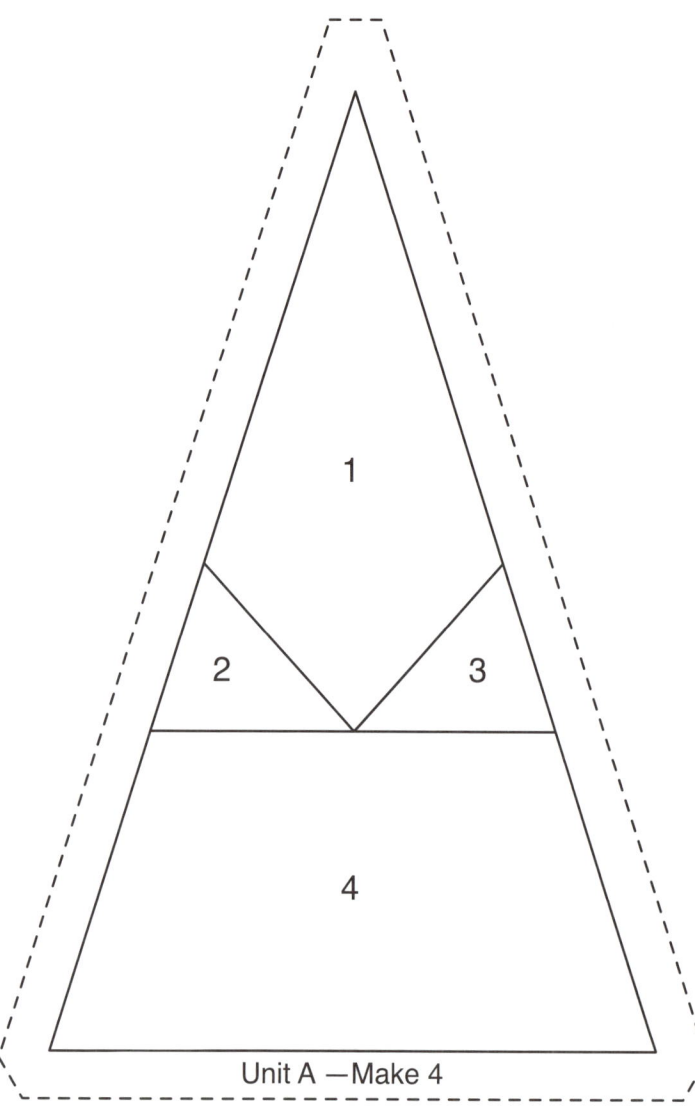

POSITION CHART

FABRIC	POSITION	SIZE
Unit A–Make 4		
Medium	1	3¼" x 4¼"
Background	2, 3	2¾" x 2¾" ◢
Background	4	2½" x 4½"
Unit B–Make 4		
Background	1	2½" x 3¼"
Medium	2, 3	1¾" x 2¼"
Dark	4	3" x 5½"
Unit C–Make 4		
Background	1	2½" x 3¼"
Medium	2, 3	1¾" x 2¼"
Unit D–Make 4		
Background	1	5¼" x 5¼" ◢

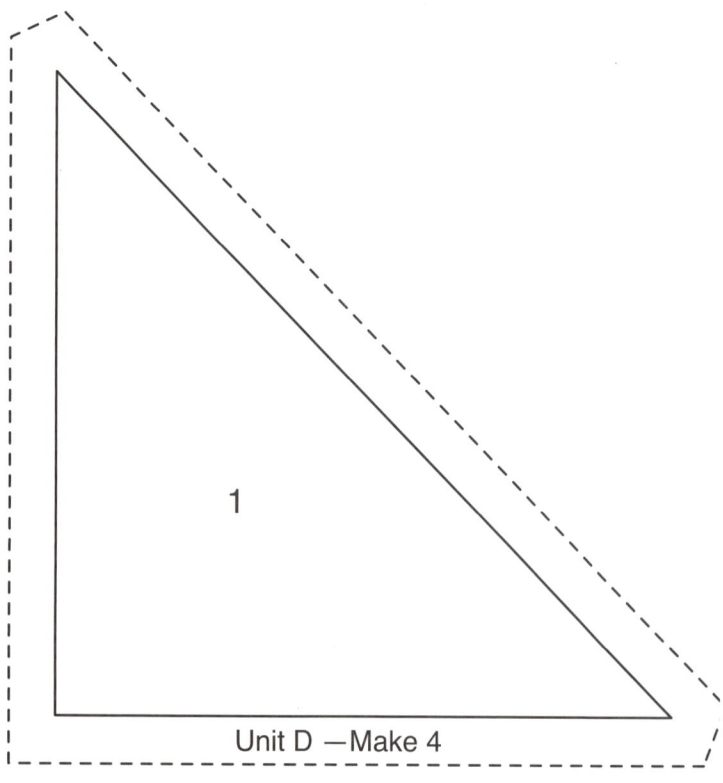

The Kaleidoscope

AUGUST 1930 • 10" BLOCK

CUTTING INSTRUCTIONS

FROM THE BACKGROUND FABRIC, CUT:

1 – 4¼" x 17" strip. Cut the strip into 4 – 4¼" squares.

1 – 3¾" x 7½" strip. Cut the strip into 2 – 3¾" squares. Cut the squares into half-square triangles.

1 – 2½" x 25" strip. Cut the strip into 10 – 2½" squares. Cut the squares into half-square triangles.

FROM THE MEDIUM FABRIC, CUT:

1 – 4¼" square.

1 – 2½" x 30" strip. Cut the strip into 12 – 2½" squares. Cut the square into half-square triangles.

FROM THE DARK FABRIC, CUT:

1 – 2½" x 5" strip. Cut the strip into 2 – 2½" squares. Cut the square into half-square triangles.

ASSEMBLING THE BLOCK

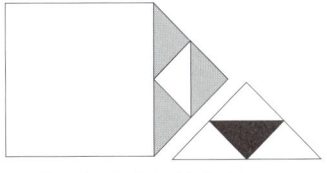
Sew Units B to Units C

Sew Units A to Units BC

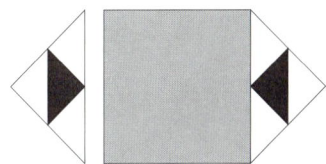
Sew Unit C to Unit F

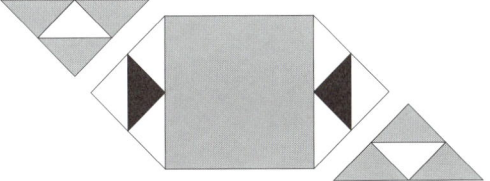
Sew Units E to Unit CF

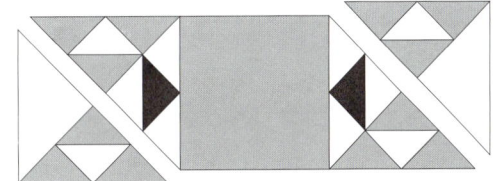
Sew Units D to Unit CEF

Assembling instructions continued on page 22.

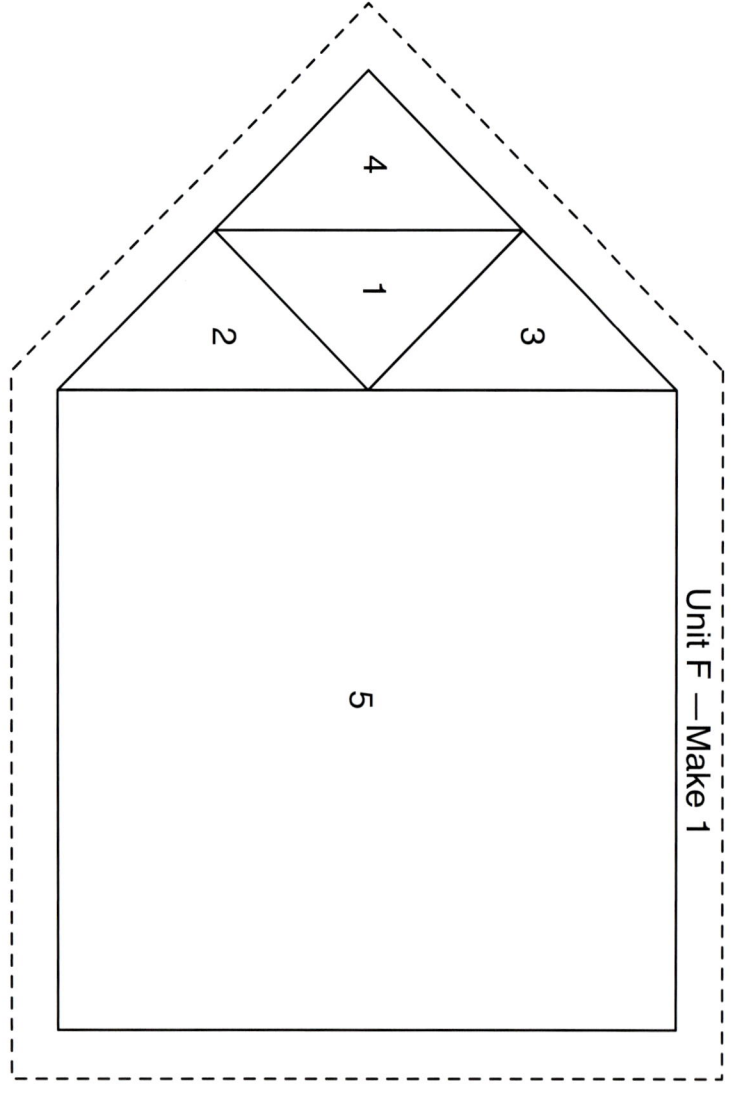

POSITION CHART

FABRIC	POSITION	SIZE	
Unit A–Make 2			
Background	1	2½" x 2½"	◣
Medium	2, 3, 4	2½" x 2½"	◣
Background	5	4¼" x 4¼"	
Background	6	3¾" x 3¾"	◣
Unit B–Make 2			
Background	1	2½" x 2½"	◣
Medium	2, 3, 4	2½" x 2½"	◣
Background	5	4¼" x 4¼"	
Unit C–Make 3			
Dark	1	2½" x 2½"	◣
Background	2, 3, 4	2½" x 2½"	◣
Unit D–Make 2			
Background	1	2½" x 2½"	◣
Medium	2, 3, 4	2½" x 2½"	◣
Background	5	3¾" x 3¾"	◣
Unit E–Make 2			
Background	1	2½" x 2½"	◣
Medium	2, 3, 4	2½" x 2½"	◣
Unit F–Make 1			
Dark	1	2½" x 2½"	◣
Background	2, 3, 4	2½" x 2½"	◣
Medium	5	4¼" x 4¼"	

ASSEMBLING THE BLOCK

Assembling instructions continued from page 21.

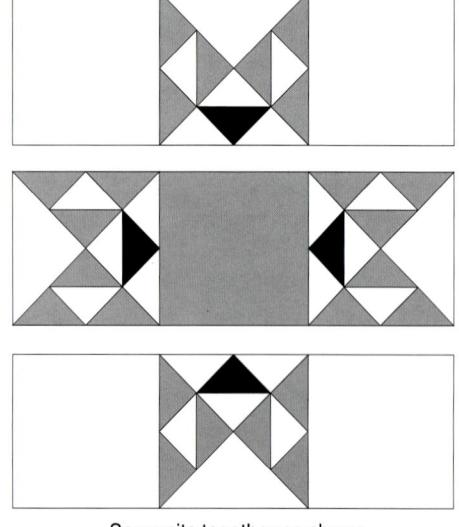

Sew units together as shown

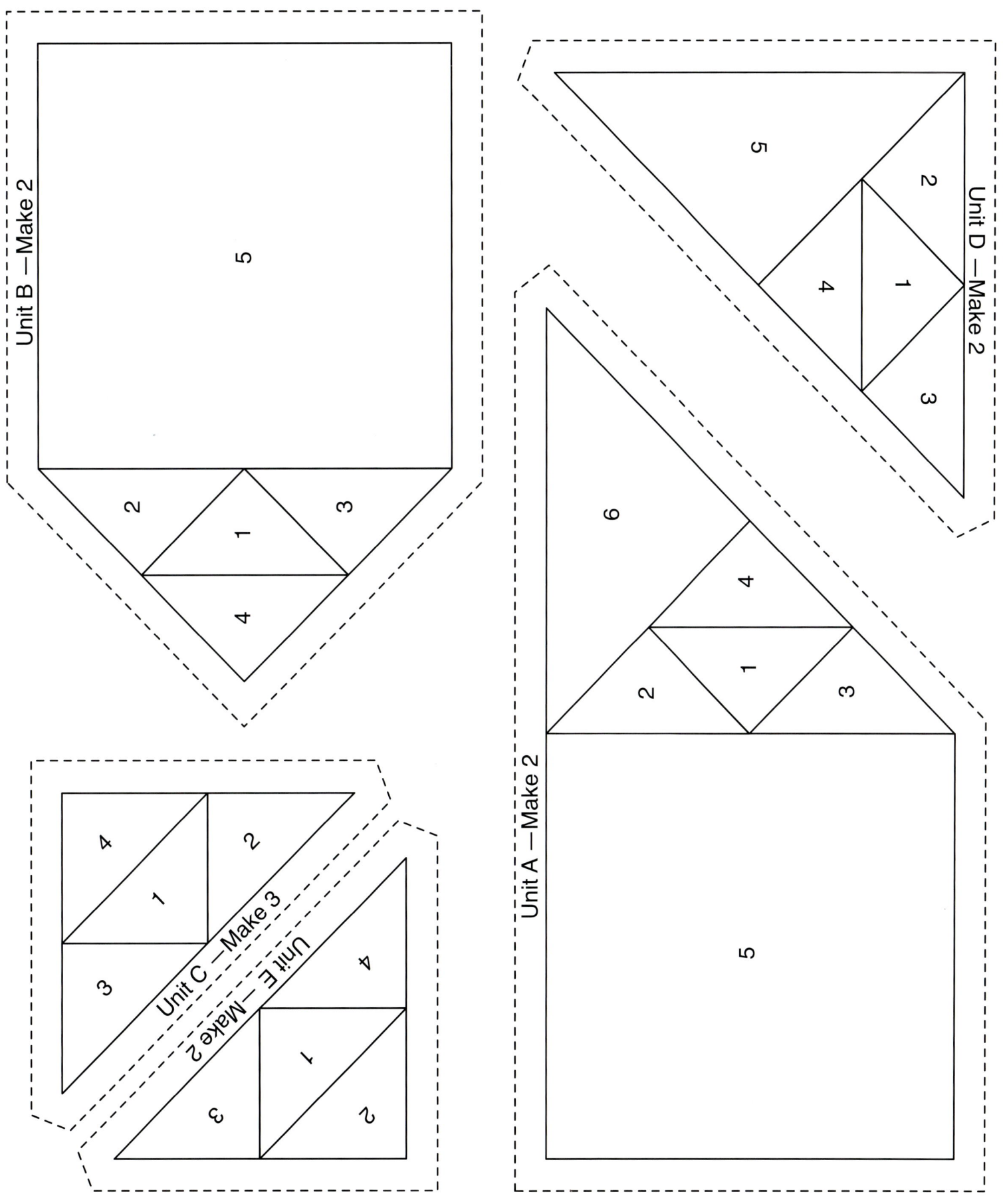

Feathered Edge Star

1934 • 10" BLOCK

CUTTING INSTRUCTIONS

FROM THE BACKGROUND FABRIC, CUT:

1 – 4¼" x 21¼" strip. Cut the strip into 5 – 4¼" squares. Cut **one** of the squares into a half-square triangle.

1 – 3" x 6" strip. Cut the strip into 2 – 3" squares.

1 – 2" x 40" and 1 – 2" x 20" strip. Cut the strips into 30 – 2" squares. Cut the squares into half-square triangles.

FROM THE MEDIUM FABRIC, CUT:

1 – 3¼" x 6½" strip. Cut the strip into 2 – 3¼" squares. Cut the squares into half-square triangles.

1 – 2" x 40 strip. Cut the strip into 20 – 2" squares. Cut the squares into half-square triangles.

1 – 1½" x 30" strip. Cut the strip into 8 – 1½" x 2¼" rectangles and 8 – 1½" x 1½" squares.

FROM THE DARK FABRIC, CUT:

1 – 3¼" x 16¼" strip. Cut the strip into 5 – 3¼" squares. Cut **four** of the squares into half-square triangles.

ASSEMBLING THE BLOCK

Sew Units A to Units B

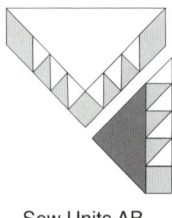
Sew Units AB to Units C

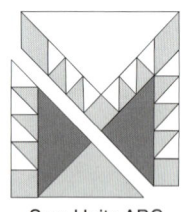
Sew Units ABC to Units D

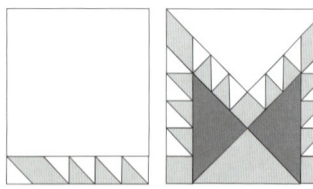
Sew Units ABCD to Units E

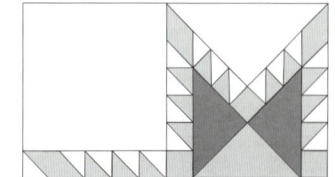
Sew Units ABCDE to Units F

ASSEMBLING THE BLOCK

Continued

Sew Units G to Units H

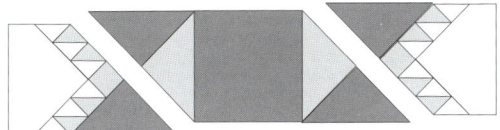

Sew Units GH to Unit I

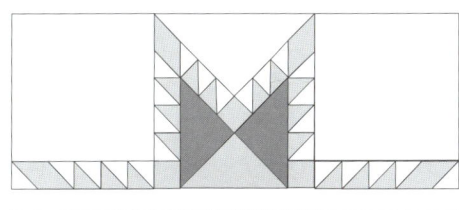

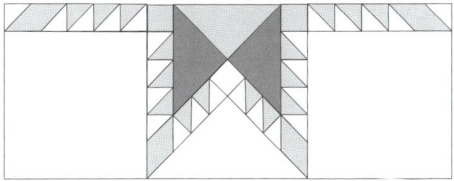

Sew together as shown

POSITION CHART

FABRIC	POSITION	SIZE	
Unit A–Make 2			
Medium	1	1½" x 2¼"	
Background	2, 4, 6	2" x 2"	◤
Medium	3, 5	2" x 2"	◤
Background	7	4¼" x 4¼"	
Unit B–Make 2			
Medium	1	1½" x 2¼"	
Background	2, 4, 6	2" x 2"	◤
Medium	3, 5	2" x 2"	◤
Medium	7	1½" x 1½"	
Unit C–Make 2			
Medium	1	1½" x 1½"	
Background	2, 4, 6, 8	2" x 2"	◤
Medium	3, 5, 7	2" x 2"	◤
Dark	9	3¼" x 3¼"	◤
Unit D–Make 2			
Medium	1	1½" x 1½"	
Background	2, 4, 6, 8	2" x 2"	◤
Medium	3, 5, 7	2" x 2"	◤
Dark	9	3¼" x 3¼"	◤
Medium	10	3¼" x 3¼"	◤
Unit E and F–Make 2 of each			
Medium	1	1½" x 2¼"	
Background	2, 3, 5, 7, 9	2" x 2"	◤
Medium	4, 6, 8	2" x 2"	◤
Background	10	4¼" x 4¼"	
Unit G–Make 2			
Medium	1	1½" x 1¼"	
Background	2, 4, 6	2" x 2"	◤
Medium	3, 5	2" x 2"	◤
Dark	7	3¼" x 3¼"	◤
Unit H–Make 2			
Background	1, 3, 5	2" x 2"	◤
Medium	2, 4	2" x 2"	◤
Background	6	3" x 3"	
Unit I–Make 1			
Dark	1	3¼" x 3¼"	
Medium	2, 3	3¼" x 3¼"	◤
Dark	4, 5	3¼" x 3¼"	◤

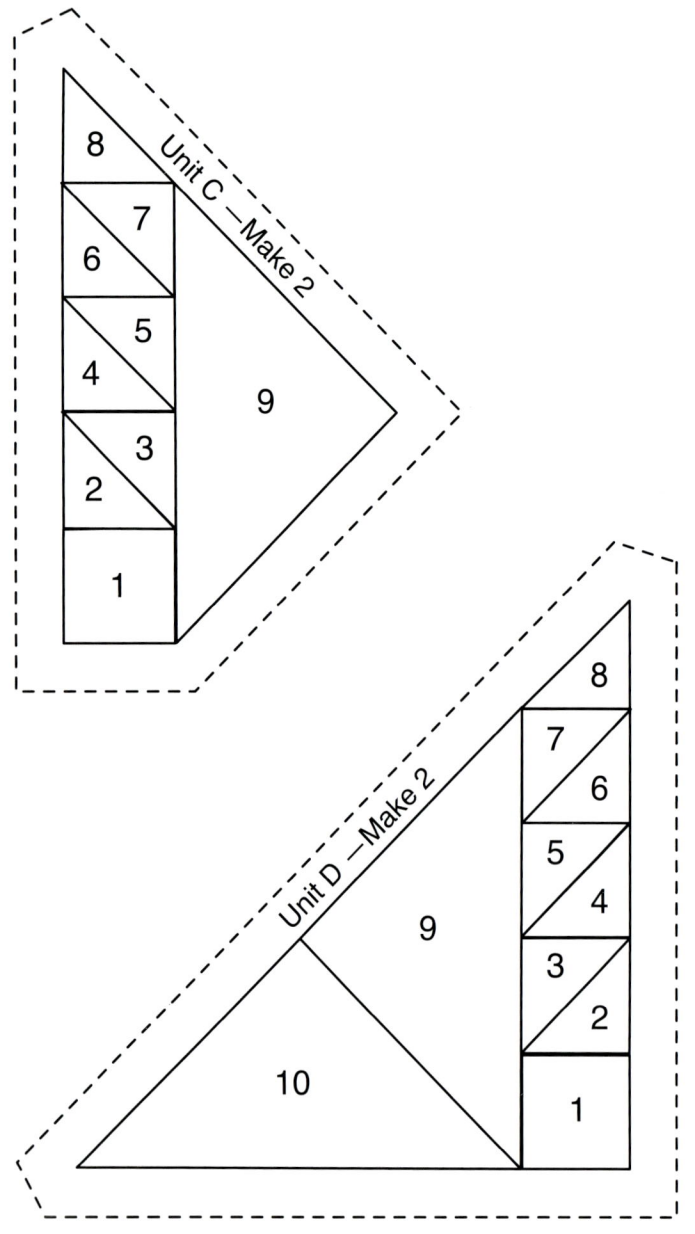
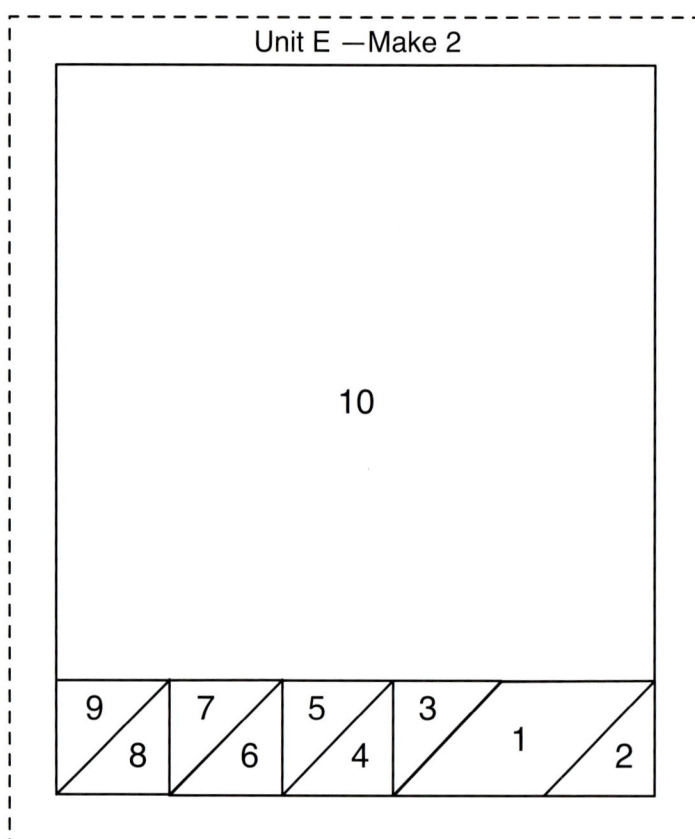
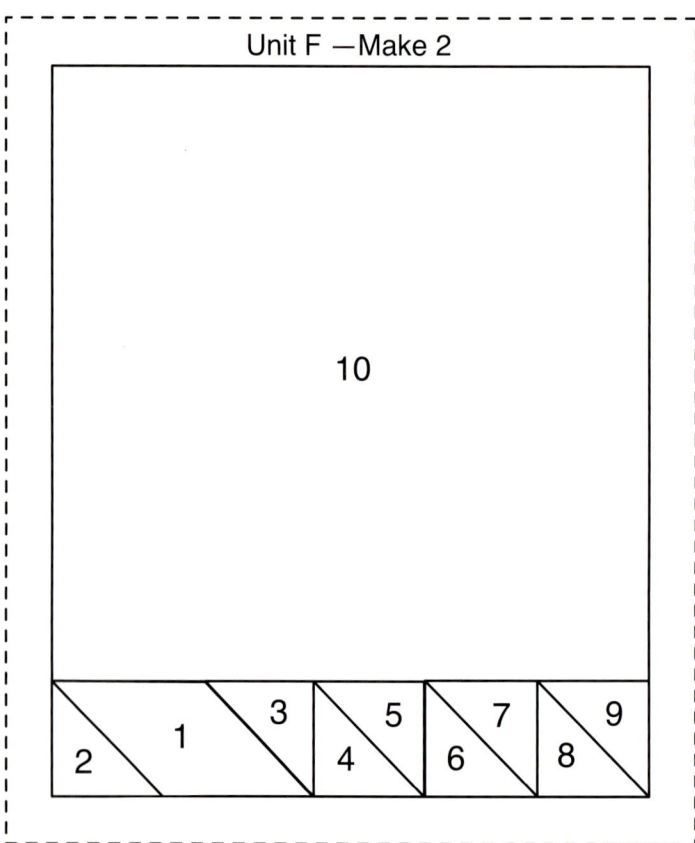

26 | HARD TIMES, SPLENDID QUILTS

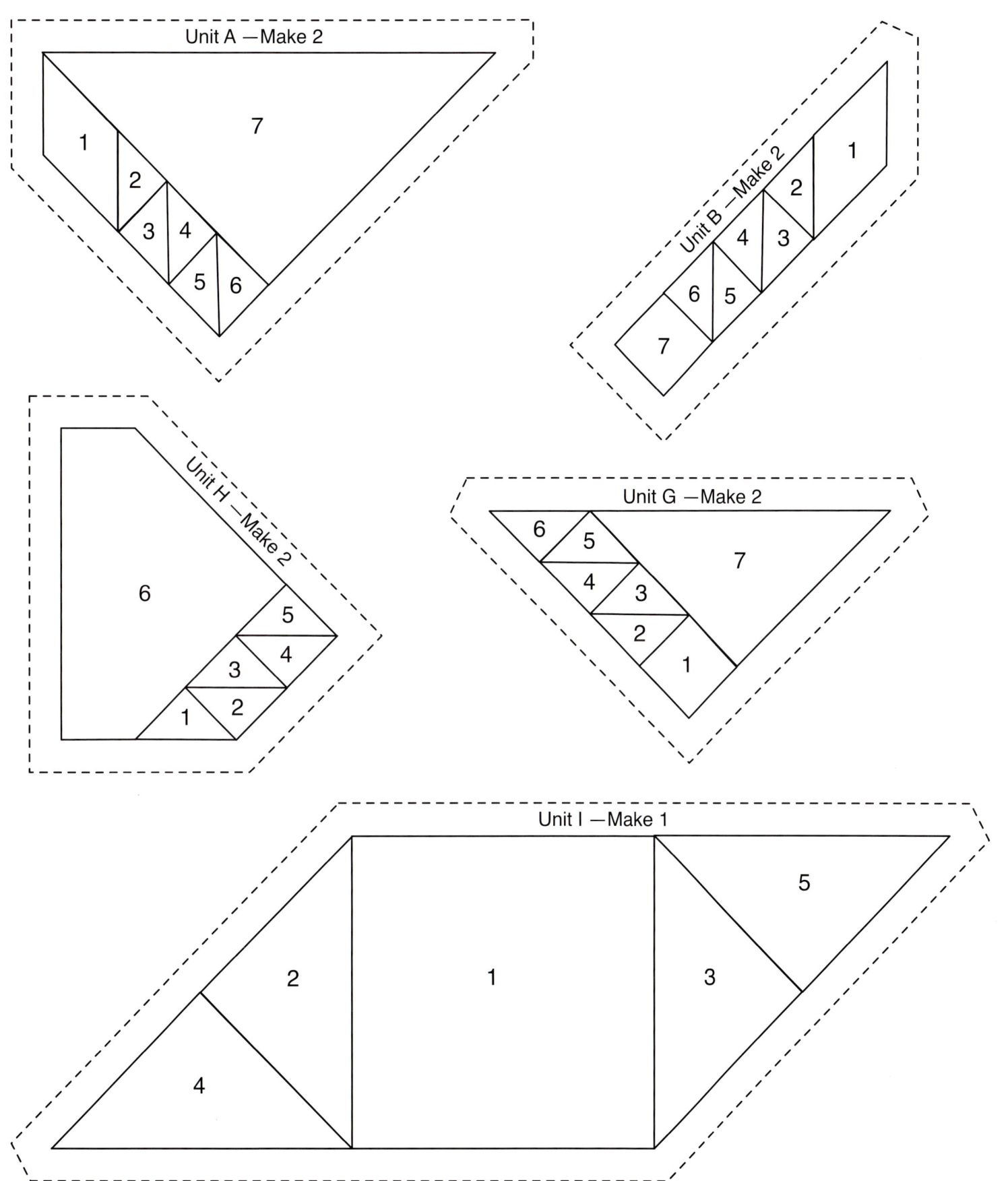

10" FEATHERED EDGE STAR | 27

The Ladies Aid Album

JANUARY 1938 • 10" BLOCK

CUTTING INSTRUCTIONS

FROM THE BACKGROUND FABRIC, CUT:

1 – 4½" x 7½" rectangle.

1 – 2½" x 18" strip. Cut the strip into 4 – 2½" x 4½" rectangles.

FROM THE MEDIUM FABRIC, CUT:

1 – 4½" x 18" strip. Cut the strip into 4 – 4½" squares.

1 – 4" square. Cut the square into half-square triangles.

FROM THE DARK FABRIC, CUT:

1 – 3" x 12" strip. Cut the strip into 4 – 3" squares. Cut the squares into half-square triangles.

ASSEMBLING THE BLOCK

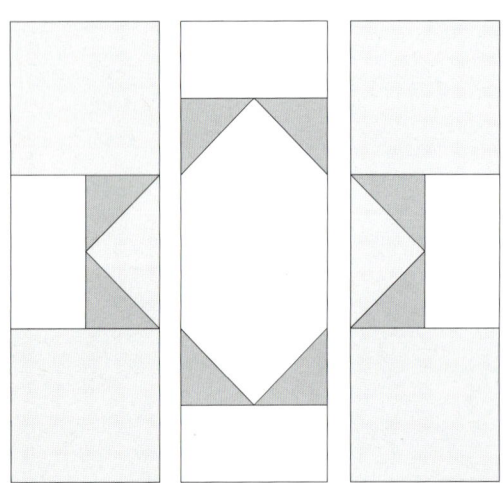

Sew each Unit B to Unit A

28 | HARD TIMES, SPLENDID QUILTS

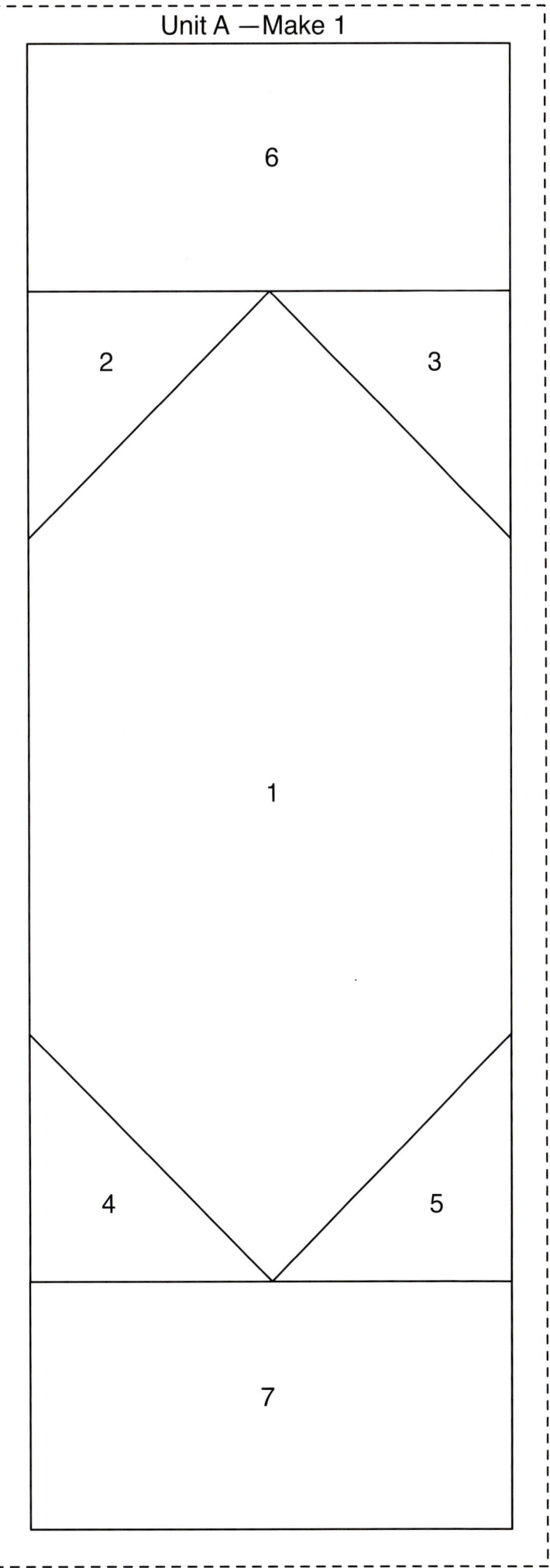

POSITION CHART

FABRIC	POSITION	SIZE
Unit A–Make 1		
Background	1	4½" x 7½"
Dark	2, 3, 4, 5	3" x 3" ◣
Background	6, 7	2½" x 4½"
Unit B–Make 2		
Medium	1	4" x 4" ◣
Dark	2, 3	3" x 3" ◣
Background	4	2½" x 4½"
Medium	5, 6	4½" x 4½"

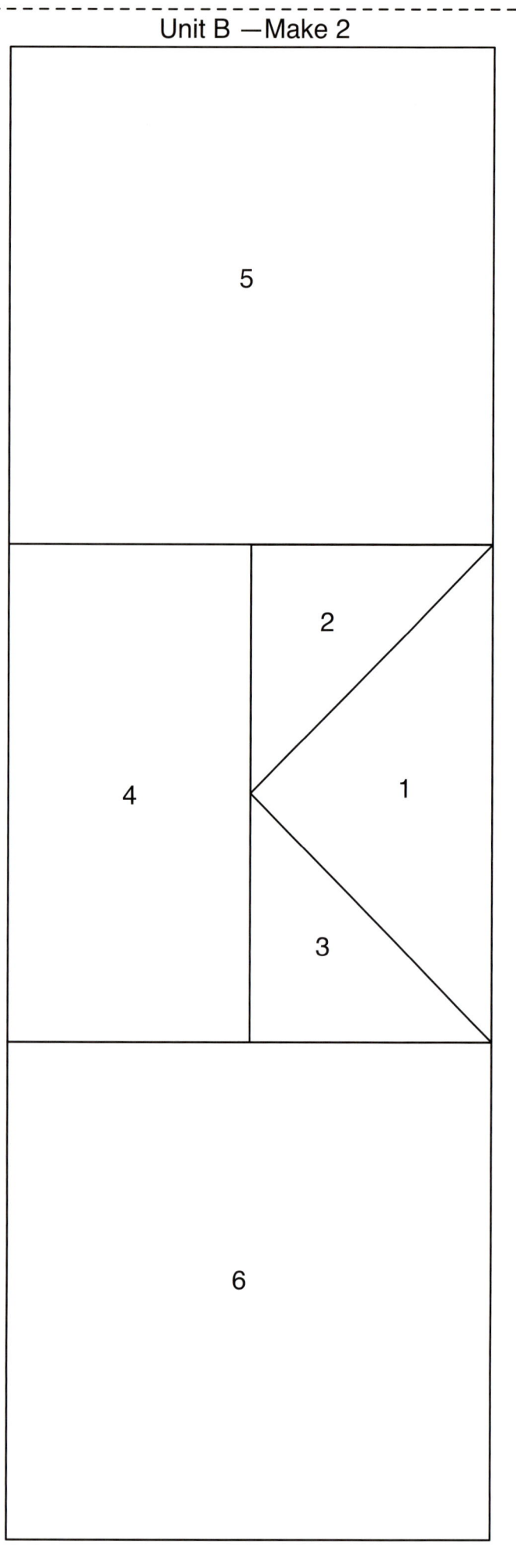

Grandmother's Favorite

NOVEMBER 1930 • 10" BLOCK

CUTTING INSTRUCTIONS

FROM THE BACKGROUND FABRIC, CUT:

1 – 6" square.

1 – 4" x 24" strip. Cut the strip into 6 – 4" squares. Cut the squares into half-square triangles.

1 – 3¼" x 6½" strip. Cut the strip into 2 – 3¼" squares. Cut the squares into half-square triangles.

FROM THE MEDIUM FABRIC, CUT:

1 – 4" x 8" strip. Cut into 2 – 4" squares. Cut the squares into half-square triangles

1 – 3¼" x 19½" strip. Cut the strip into 6 – 3¼" squares. Cut the squares into half-square triangles.

ASSEMBLING THE BLOCK

Sew Unit B to Unit C

Sew each Unit A to Unit BC

POSITION CHART

FABRIC	POSITION	SIZE
Unit A–Make 2		
Background	1	3¼" x 3¼"
Medium	2, 3, 4	3¼" x 3¼"
Background	5, 6, 9, 10	4" x 4"
Medium	7, 8	4" x 4"
Unit B–Make 1		
Background	1	3¼" x 3¼"
Medium	2, 3, 4	3¼" x 3¼"
Background	5, 6	4" x 4"
Unit C–Make 1		
Background	1	3¼" x 3¼"
Medium	2, 3, 4	3¼" x 3¼"
Background	5, 6	4" x 4"
Background	7	6" x 6"

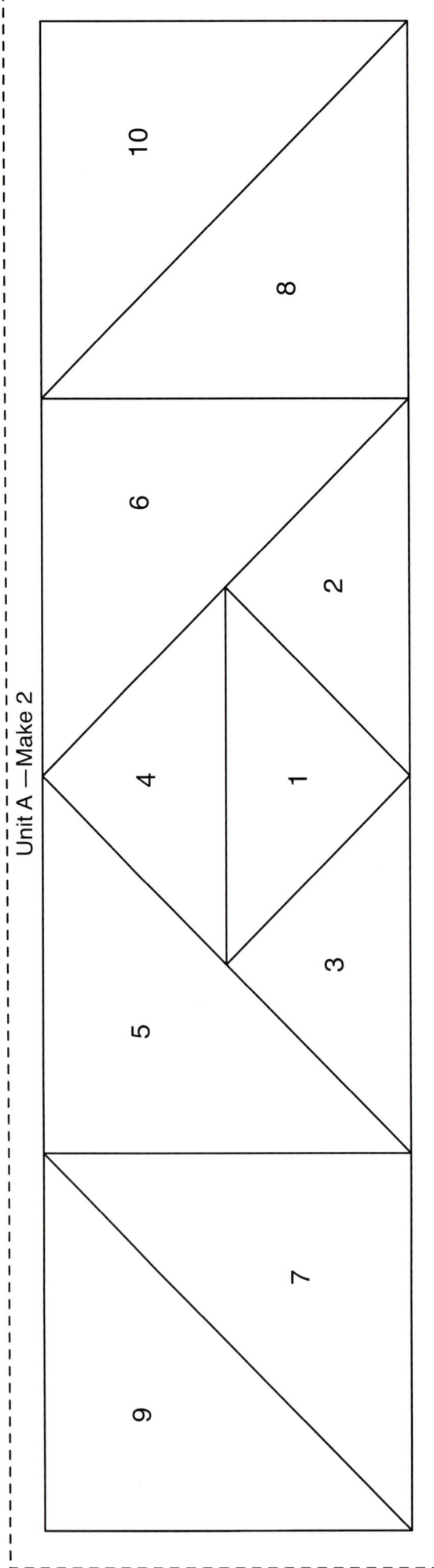

Unit A —Make 2

Unit C —Make 1

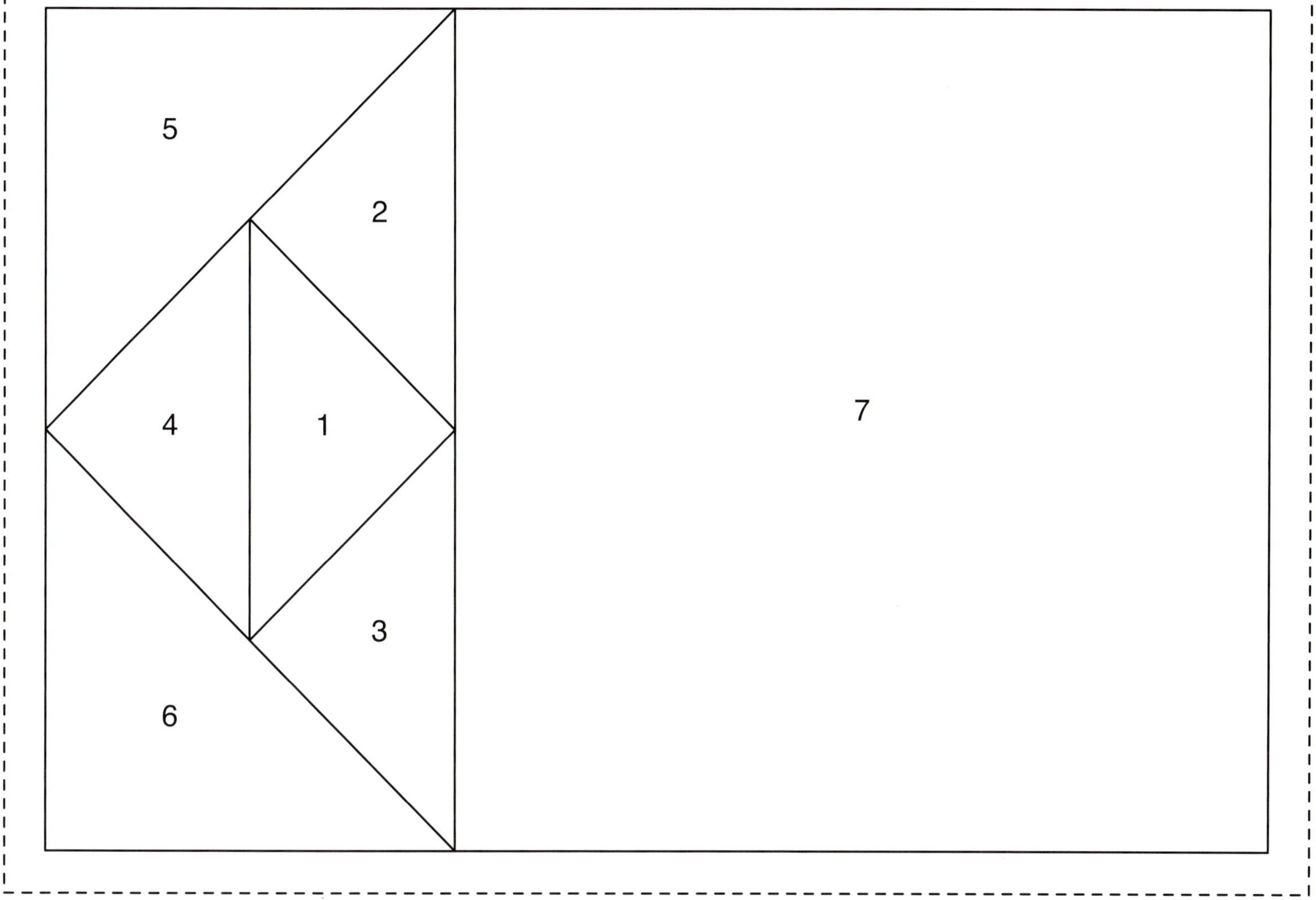

Unit B —Make 1

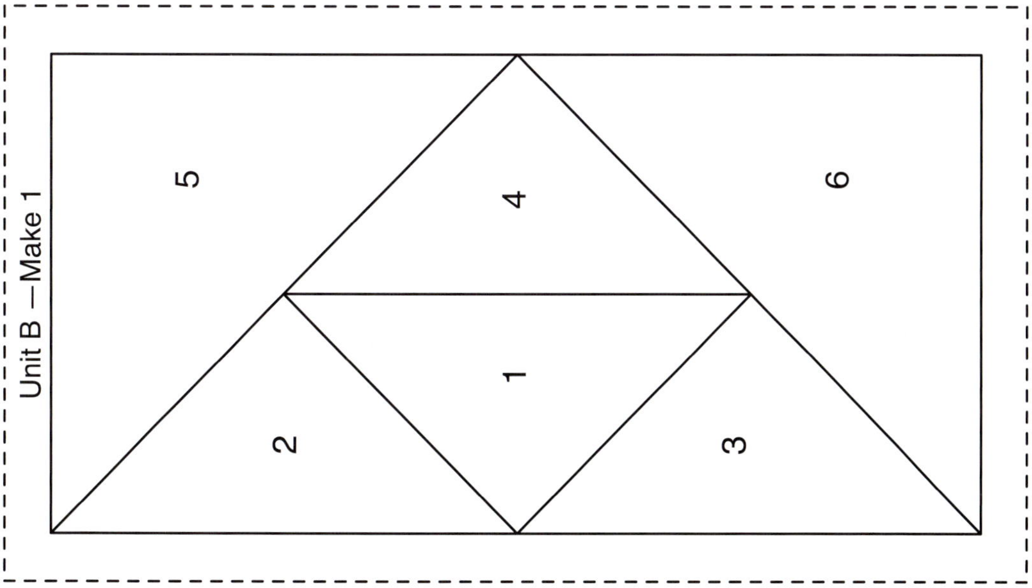

10" GRANDMOTHER'S FAVORITE | 33

The Pine Burr

AUGUST 1939 • 10" BLOCK

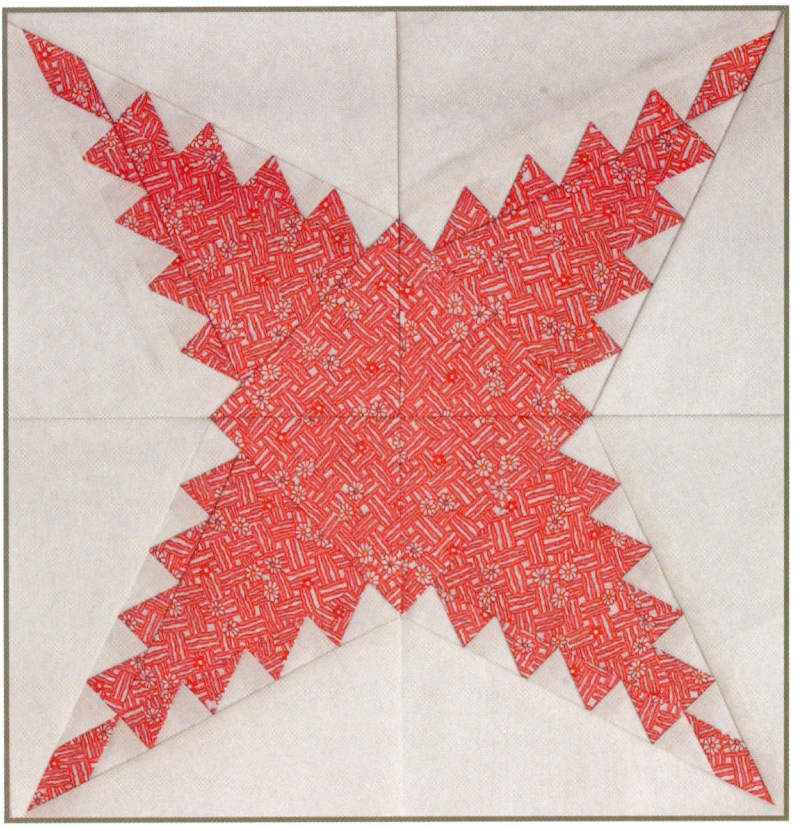

CUTTING INSTRUCTIONS

FROM THE BACKGROUND FABRIC, CUT:

1 – 3½" x 24" strip. Cut the strip into 4 – 3½" x 6" rectangles.

1 – 3¼" x 26" strip. Cut the strip into 4 – 3¼" x 6½" rectangles.

2 – 1¾" x 35" strips. Cut the strips into 40 – 1¾" squares.

FROM THE MEDIUM FABRIC, CUT:

1 – 4¼" x 8½" strip. Cut the strip into 2 – 4¼" squares. Cut the squares into half-square triangles.

1 – 3¼" x 20" strip. Cut the strip into 4 – 3¼" x 5" rectangles

1 – 1¾" x 38½" strip and 1 – 1¾" x 17½" strip. Cut the strips into 32 – 1¾" squares.

1 – 1¼" x 12" strip. Cut the strip into 4 – 1¼" x 3" rectangles.

ASSEMBLING THE BLOCK

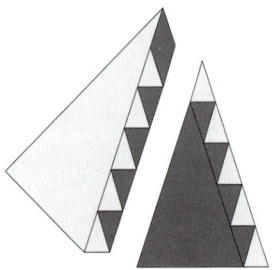

Sew each Unit A to a Unit B

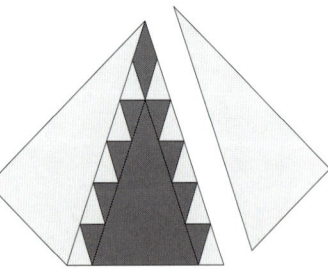

Sew each Unit C to a Unit AB

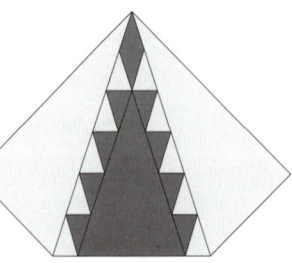

Sew each Unit D to a Unit ABC

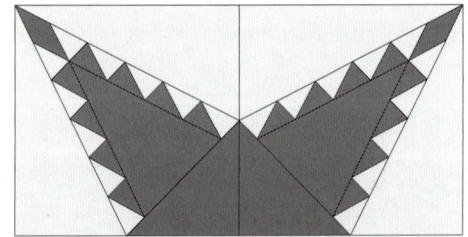

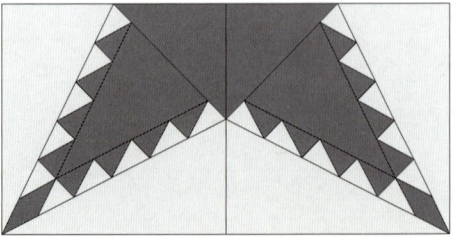

Complete block as shown

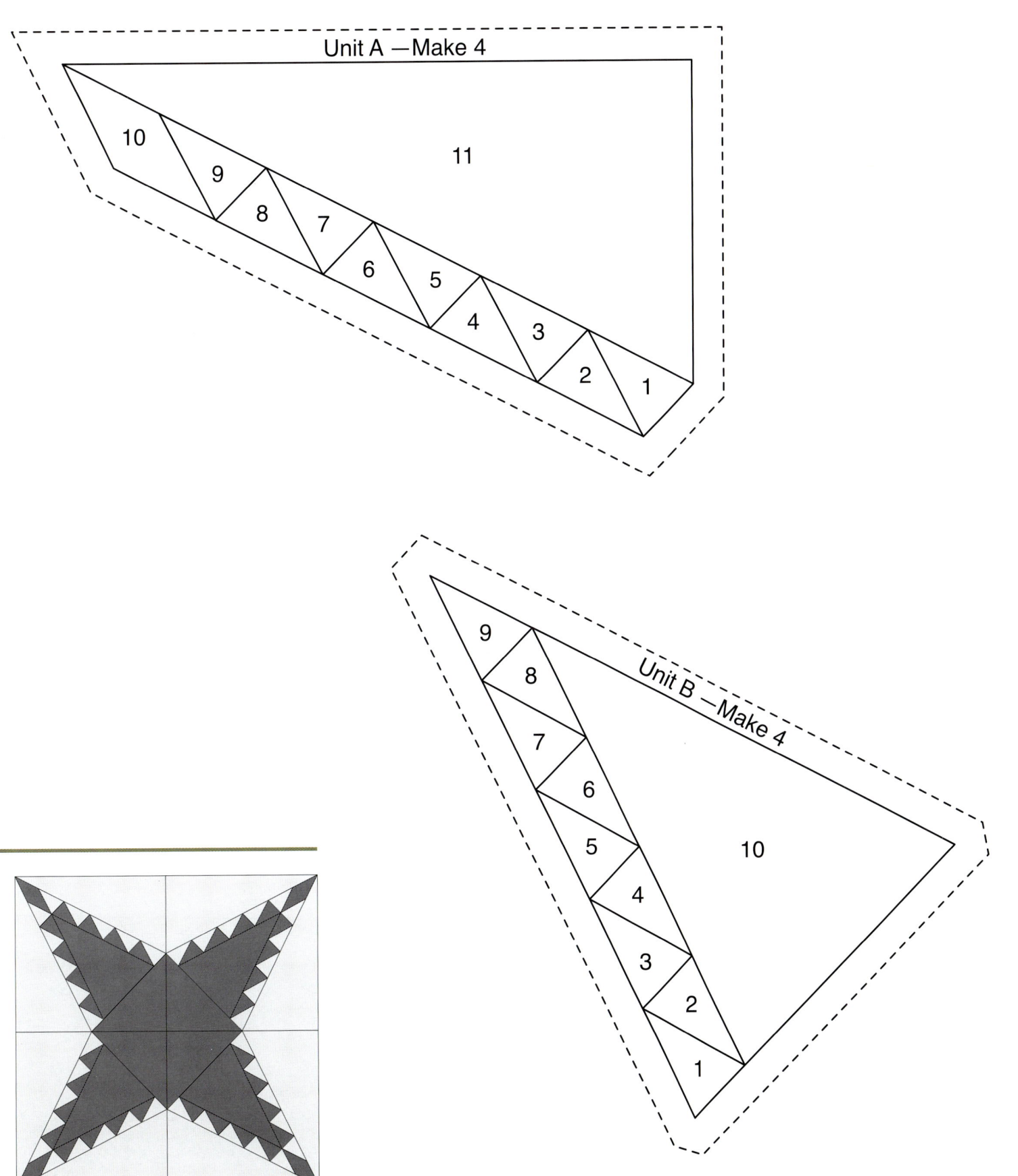

10" THE PINE BURR

POSITION CHART

FABRIC	POSITION	SIZE
Unit A–Make 4		
Background	1, 3, 5, 7, 9	1¾" x 1¾"
Medium	2, 4, 6, 8	1¾" x 1¾"
Medium	10	1¼" x 3"
Background	11	3¼" x 6½"
Unit B–Make 4		
Background	1, 3, 5, 7, 9	1¾" x 1¾"
Medium	2, 4, 6, 8	1¾" x 1¾"
Medium	10	3¼" x 5"
Unit C–Make 4		
Background	1	3½" x 6"
Unit D–Make 4		
Medium	1	4¼" x 4¼"

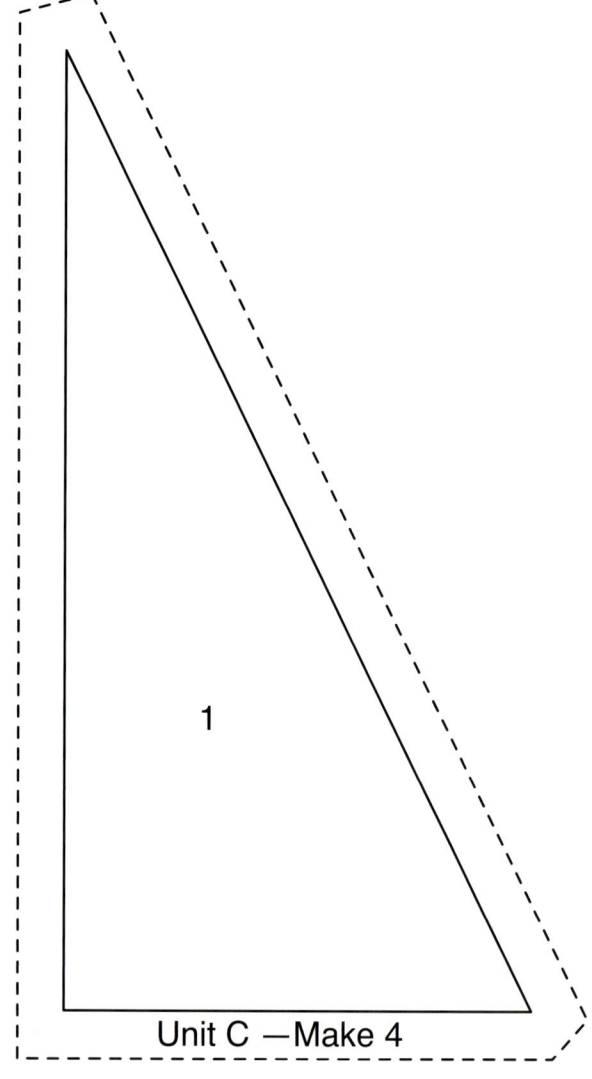

Unit C —Make 4

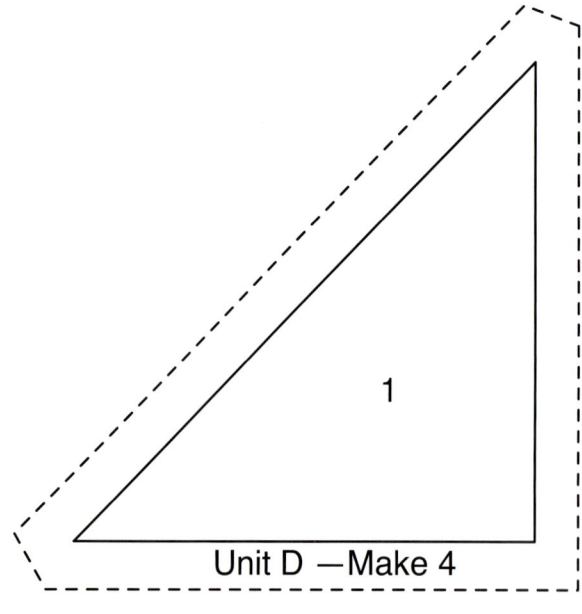

Unit D —Make 4

The Christmas Tree

DECEMBER 1932 • 10" BLOCK

CUTTING INSTRUCTIONS

FROM THE BACKGROUND FABRIC, CUT:

1 – 6½" x 22½" strip. Cut the strip into 2 – 6½" x 11¼" rectangles.

1 – 2½" x 19" strip. Cut the strip into 4 – 2½" squares and 2 – 2½" x 4½" rectangles.

1 – 1¾" x 40" strip and 1 – 1¾" x 10" strip. Cut the strips into 20 – 1¾" x 2½" rectangles.

FROM THE MEDIUM FABRIC, CUT:

1 – 2½" square.

1 – 1¾" x 7½" strip. Cut the strip into 3 – 1¾" x 2½" rectangles.

1 – 1½" x 38½" strip and 1 – 1½" x 16½" strip. Cut the strips into 20 – 1½" x 2¾" rectangles.

ASSEMBLING THE BLOCK

Sew Unit A to Unit B

Sew Unit C to Unit D

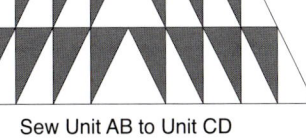

Sew Unit AB to Unit CD

Sew Unit E to Unit ABCD

Assembling instructions continued on page 38.

POSITION CHART

FABRIC	POSITION	SIZE
Unit A–Make 1		
Background	1	2½" x 2½"
Medium	2, 4, 6, 8, 10, 12, 14, 16	1½" x 2¾"
Background	3, 5, 7, 9, 11, 13, 15, 17	1¾" x 2½"
Unit B–Make 1		
Background	1	2½" x 2½"
Medium	2, 4, 6, 8, 10, 12	1½" x 2¾"
Background	3, 5, 7, 9, 11, 13	1¾" x 2½"
Unit C–Make 1		
Background	1	2½" x 2½"
Medium	2, 4, 6, 8	1½" x 2¾"
Background	3, 5, 7, 9	1¾" x 2½"
Unit D–Make 1		
Background	1	2½" x 2½"
Medium	2, 4	1½" x 2¾"
Background	3, 5	1¾" x 2½"
Medium	6	2½" x 2½"
Unit E–Make 1		
Medium	1	1¾" x 2½"
Background	2, 3	2½" x 4½"
Medium	4, 5	1¾" x 2½"
Units F & G–Make 1 each		
Background	1	6½" x 11¼"

ASSEMBLING THE BLOCK

Assembling instructions continued from page 37.

Sew Unit F and G to each side of Unit ABCDE

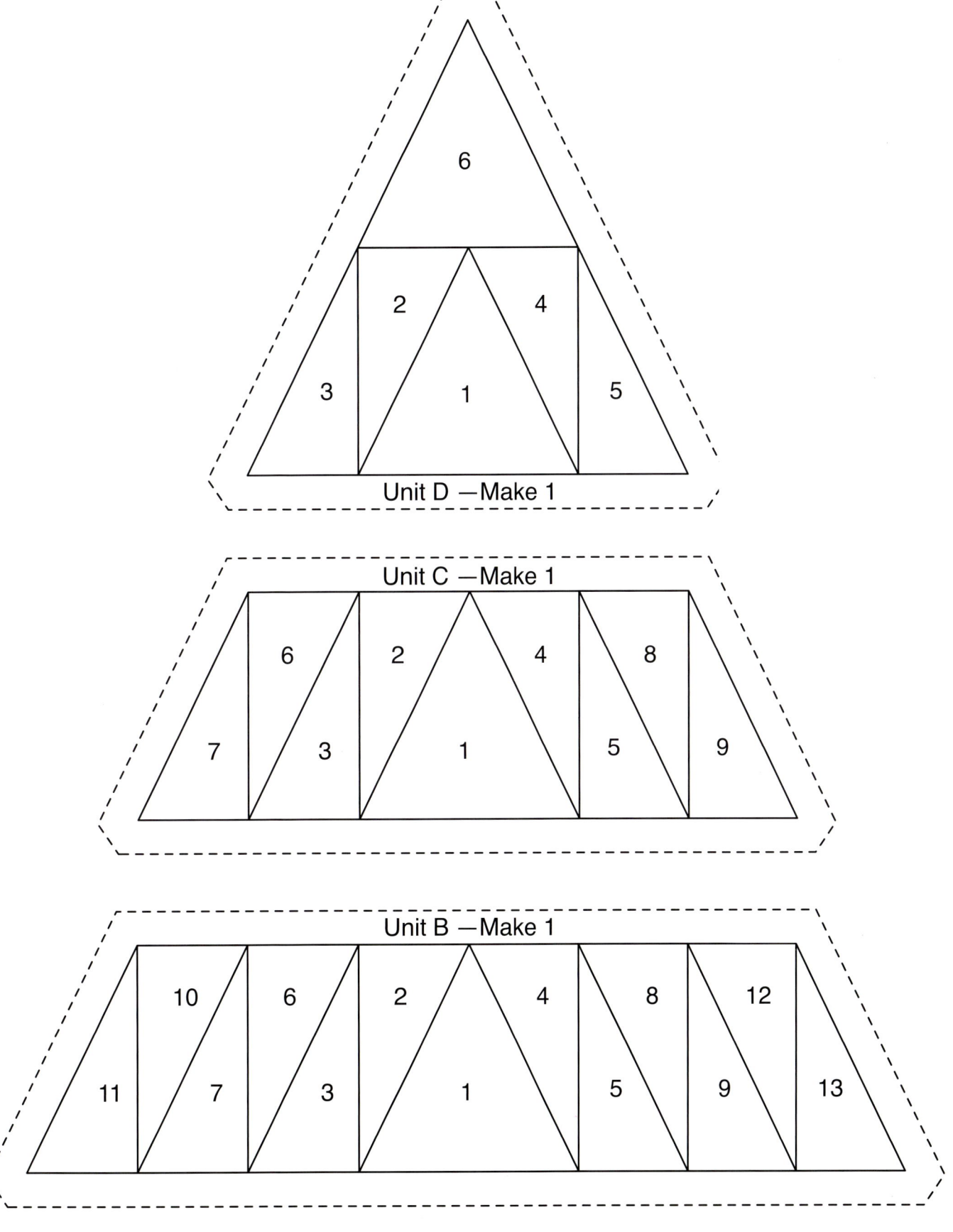

10" THE CHRISTMAS TREE | 39

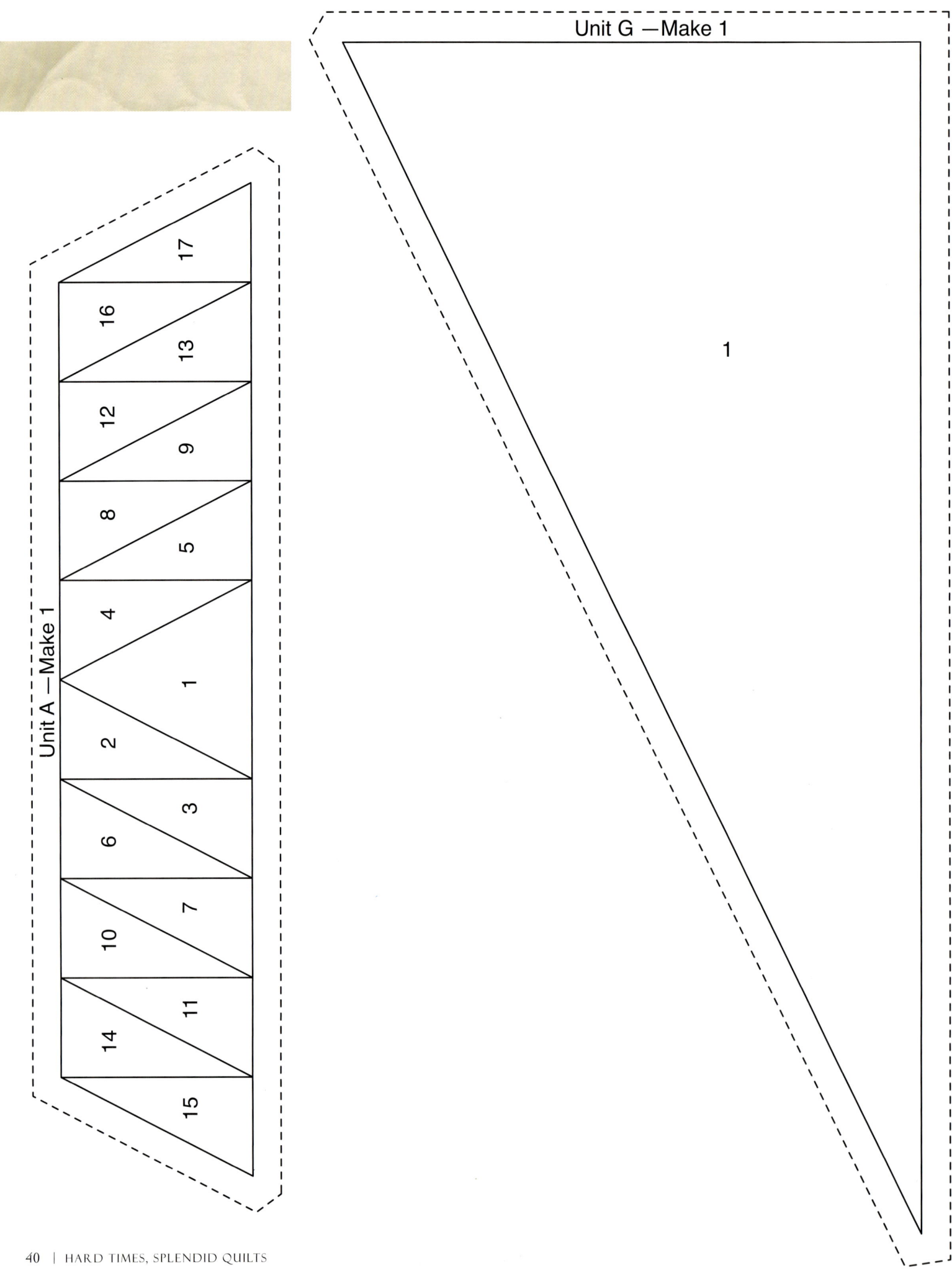

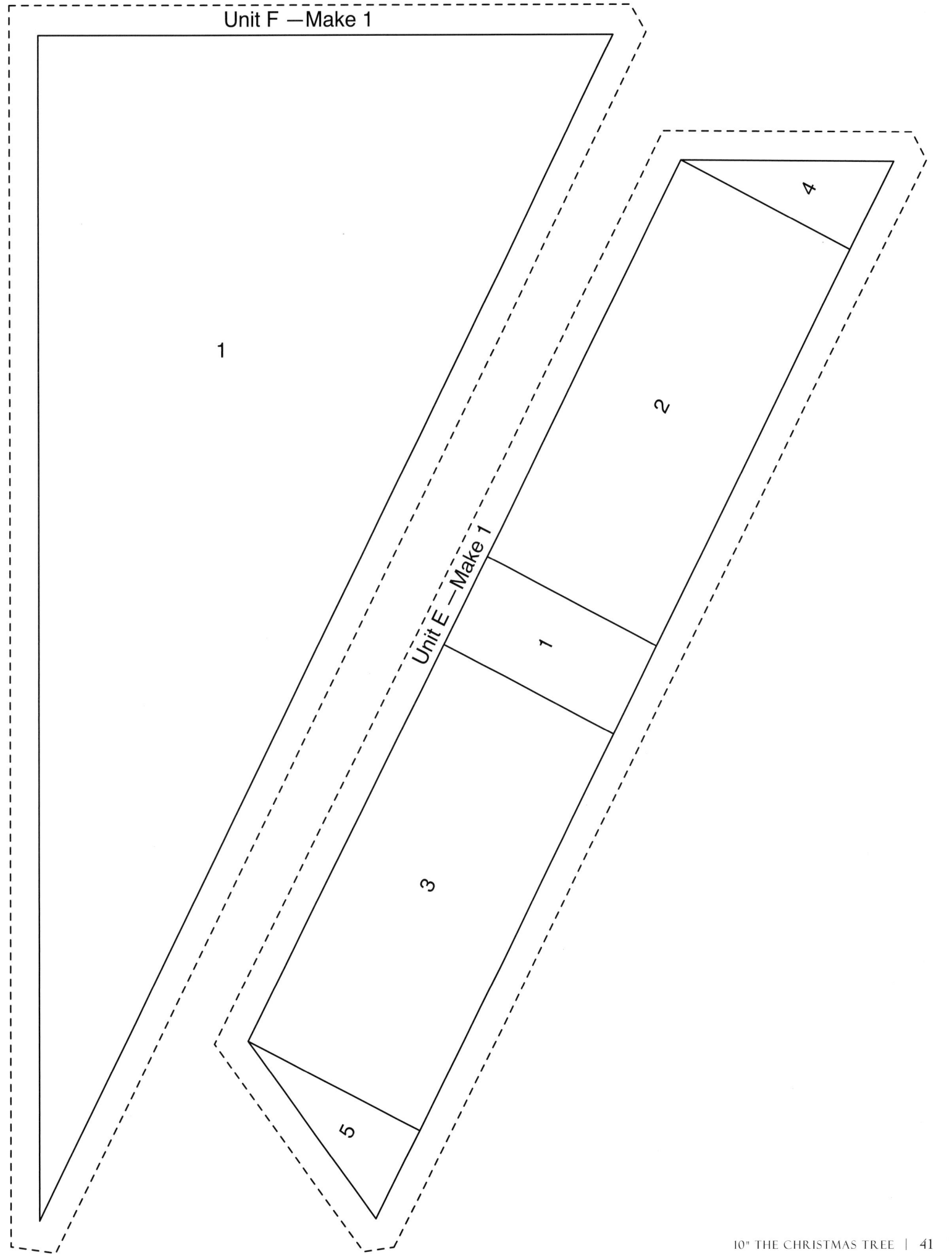

10" THE CHRISTMAS TREE | 41

The Basket

MAY 1938 • 10" BLOCK

CUTTING INSTRUCTIONS

FROM THE BACKGROUND FABRIC, CUT:

1 – 7" square. Cut the square into half-square triangles. You will have one half-square triangle left over.

1 – 5¼" square. Cut the square into half-square triangles. You will have one half-square triangle left over.

1 – 4½" x 9" strip. Cut the strip into 2 – 4½" squares. Cut the squares into half-square triangles. You will have one half-square triangle left over.

1 – 3¼" square. Cut the square into half-square triangles. You will have one half-square triangle left over.

1 – 2½" x 15½" strip. Cut the strip into 2 – 2½" x 7¾" rectangles.

1 – 1½" x 18" strip. Cut the strip into 1 – 1½" x 8½" rectangle and 1 – 1½" x 9½" rectangle.

FROM THE MEDIUM FABRIC, CUT:

1 – 4½" x 13½" strip. Cut the strip into 3 – 4½" squares. Cut the squares into half-square triangles. You will have one left over.

1 – 3¼" square. Cut the square into half-square triangles.

1 – 1½" x 19½" strip. Cut the strip into 1 – 1½" x 5" rectangle, 1 – 1½" x 7" rectangle and 1 – 1½" x 7½" rectangle.

ASSEMBLING THE BLOCK

Sew Unit B to Unit C

Sew Units D and E to Unit BC

Sew Unit F to Unit BCDE

Sew Unit A to Unit BCDEF

POSITION CHART

FABRIC	POSITION	SIZE	
Unit A–Make 1			
Background	1	7" x 7"	◤
Medium	2	1½" x 7"	
Medium	3	1½" x 7½"	
Background	4	1½" x 8½"	
Background	5	1½" x 9½"	
Unit B–Make 1			
Medium	1, 3, 5	4½" x 4½"	◤
Background	2, 4	4½" x 4½"	
Unit C–Make 1			
Medium	1, 5	4½" x 4½"	◤
Background	2	4½" x 4½"	◤
Medium	3	1½" x 5"	
Background	4	3¼" x 3¼"	◤
Unit D–Make 1			
Background	1	2½" x 7¾"	
Medium	2	3¼" x 3¼"	◤
Unit E–Make 1			
Background	1	2½" x 7¾"	
Medium	2	3¼" x 3¼"	◤
Unit F–Make 1			
Background	1	5¼" x 5¼"	◤

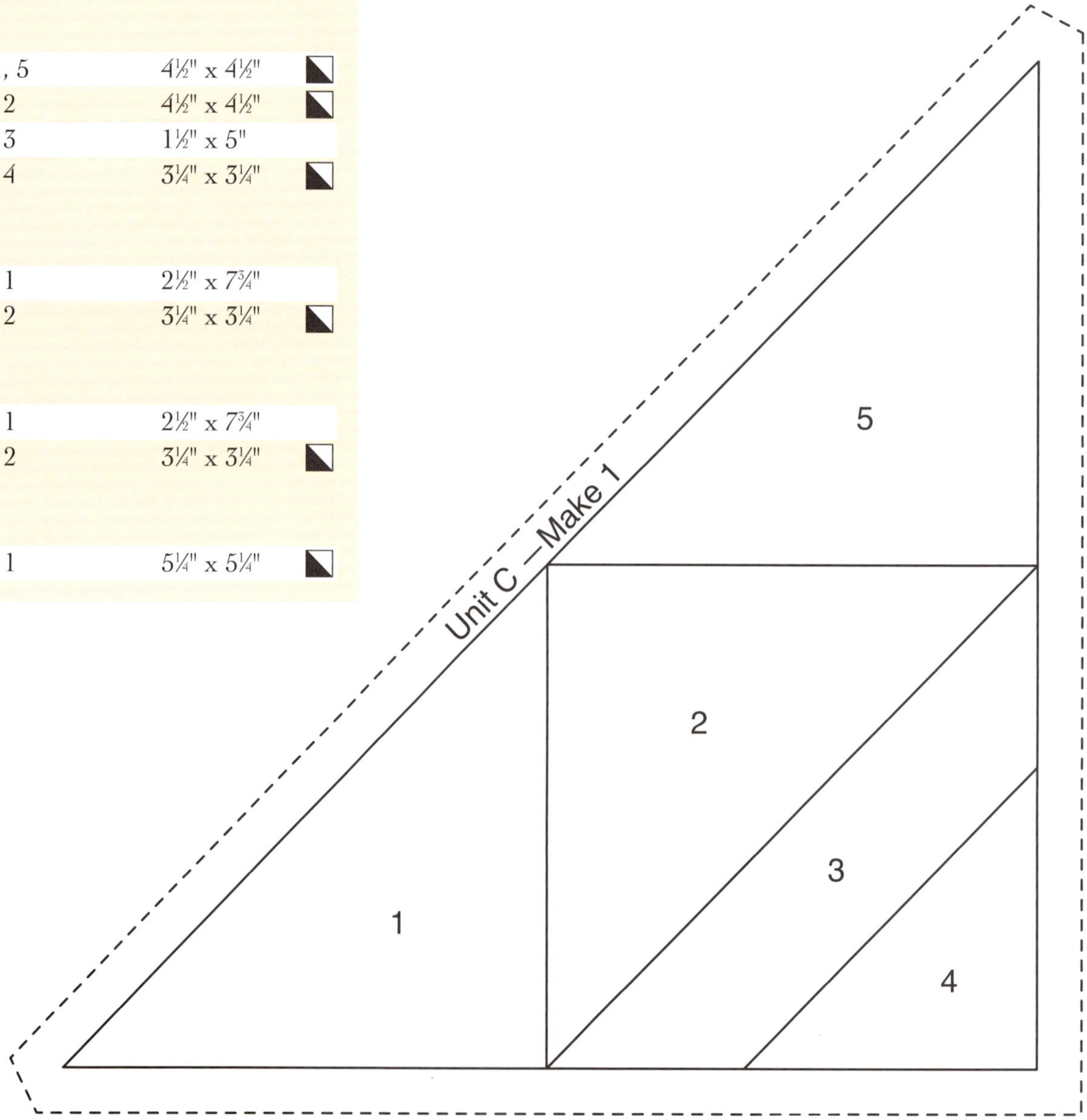

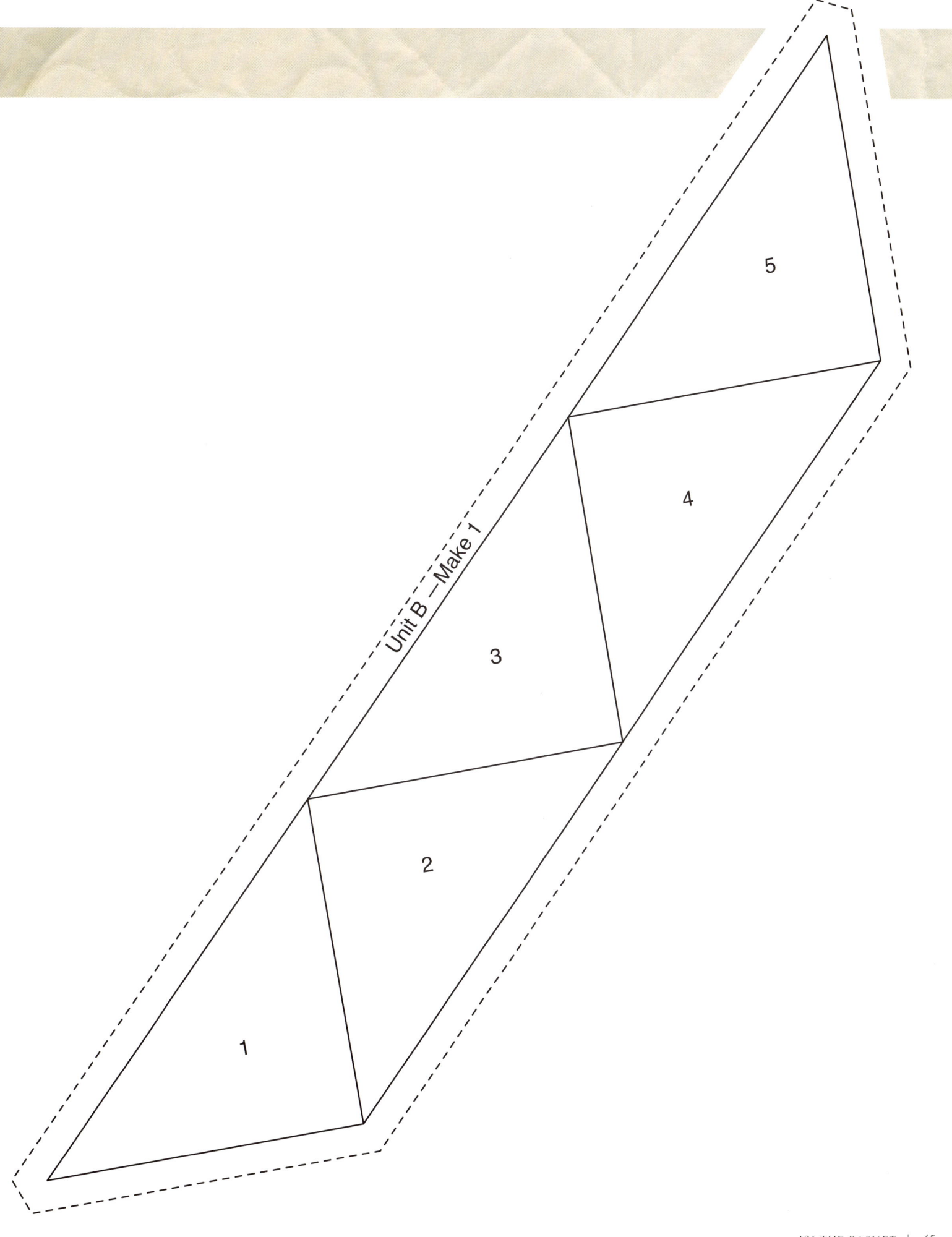

10" THE BASKET | 45

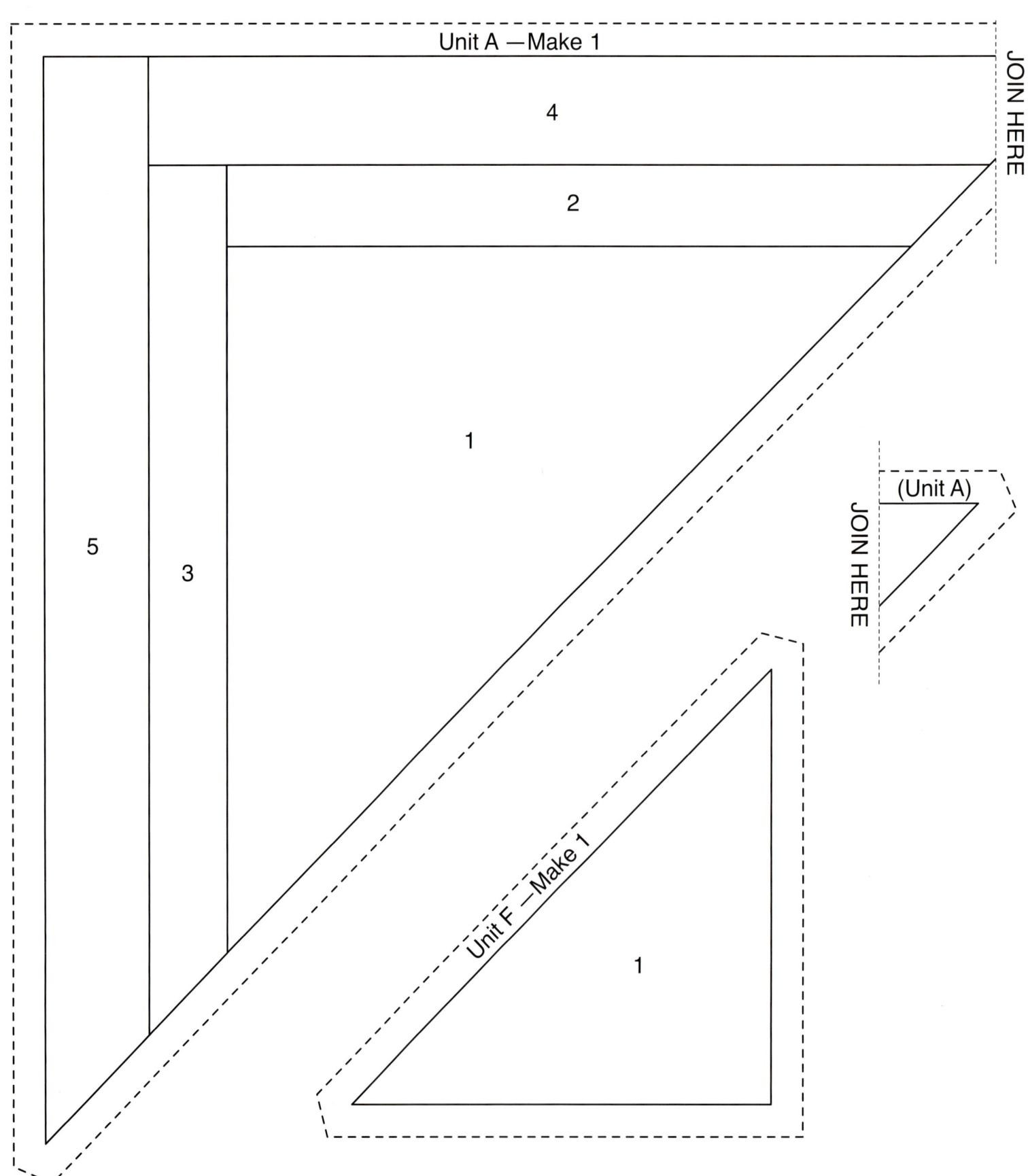

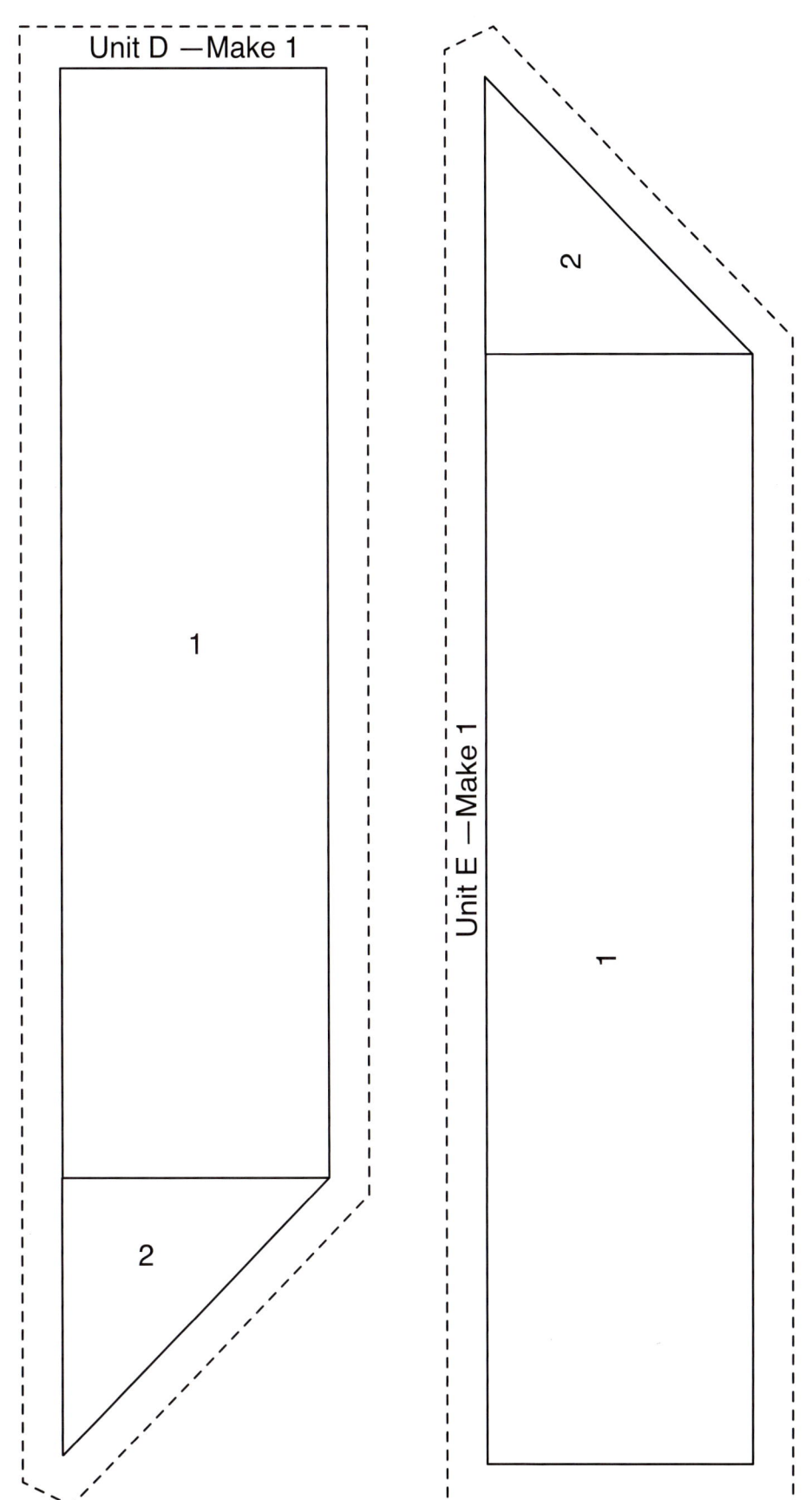

The Lone Star of Paradise

MARCH 1933 • 10" BLOCK

CUTTING INSTRUCTIONS

FROM THE BACKGROUND FABRIC, CUT:

1 – 2½" x 20" strip. Cut the strip into 8 – 2½" squares. Cut the squares into half-square triangles.

1 – 2¼" x 18" strip. Cut the strip into 8 – 2¼" squares.

FROM THE LIGHT FABRIC, CUT:

1 – 3" x 6" strip. Cut the strip into 2 – 3" squares. Cut the squares into half-square triangles.

1 – 2½" x 15" strip. Cut the strip into 6 – 2½" squares. Cut the squares into half-square triangles.

1 – 1¾" x 18" strip. Cut the strip into 8 – 1¾" x 2¼" rectangles.

FROM THE MEDIUM FABRIC, CUT:

1 – 3" x 6" strip. Cut the strip into 2 – 3" squares. Cut the squares into half-square triangles.

1 – 2½" x 5" strip. Cut the strip into 2 – 2½" squares. Cut the squares into half-square triangles.

1 – 2¼" x 18" strip. Cut the strip into 8 – 2¼" squares.

1 – 2" x 4" strip. Cut the strip into 2 – 2" squares. Cut the squares into half-square triangles.

FROM THE DARK FABRIC, CUT:

1 – 3" x 6" strip. Cut the strip into 2 – 3" squares. Cut the squares into half-square triang-es.

1 – 2¼" x 9" strip. Cut the strip into 4 – 2¼" squares.

1 – 1¾" x 37" strip. Cut the strip into 8 –1¾" x 3½" rectangles and 4 – 1¾" x 2¼" rectangles.

ASSEMBLING THE BLOCK

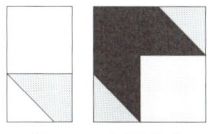
Sew each Unit A to a Unit C as shown

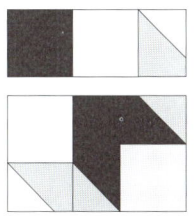
Sew each Unit B to Unit AC

Sew each Unit D to Units E

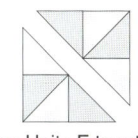
Sew Units F together

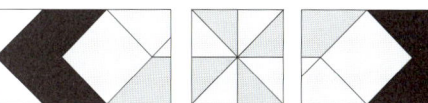
Sew Units DE to Units F

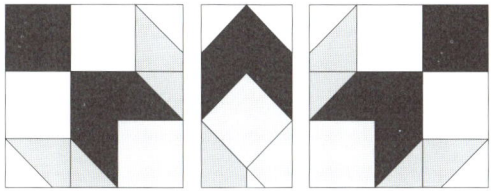
Sew Units ABC to Units DE

Sew units together as shown

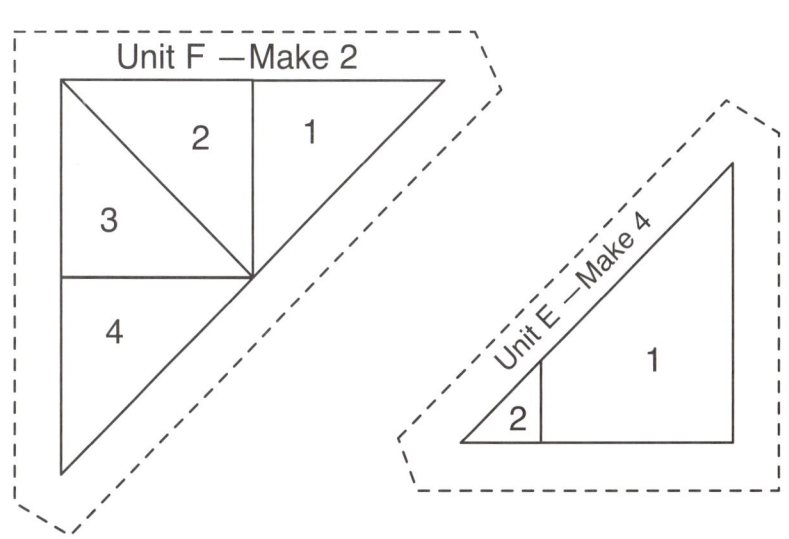

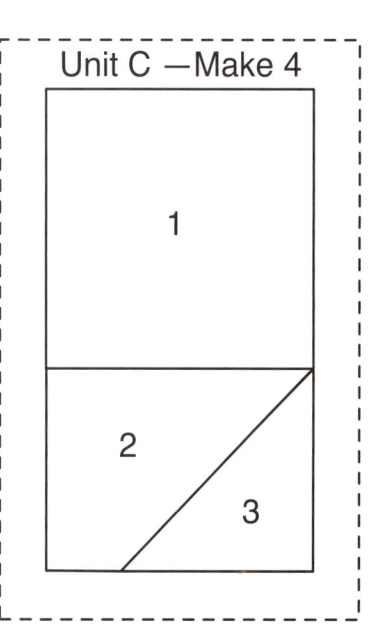

10" THE LONE STAR OF PARADISE | 49

POSITION CHART

FABRIC	POSITION	SIZE	
Unit A–Make 4			
Medium	1	2¼" x 2¼"	
Dark	2	1¾" x 2¼"	
Dark	3	1¾" x 3½"	
Light	4, 5	2½" x 2½"	◣
Unit B–Make 4			
Dark	1	2¼" x 2¼"	
Background	2	2¼" x 2¼"	
Light	3	1¾" x 2¼"	
Background	4	2½" x 2½"	◣
Unit C–Make 4			
Background	1	2¼" x 2¼"	
Light	2	1¾" x 2¼"	
Background	3	2½" x 2½"	◣
Unit D–Make 4			
Medium	1	2¼" x 2¼"	
Dark	2	3" x 3"	◣
Medium	3	3" x 3"	◣
Dark	4	1¾" x 3½"	
Background	5, 6	2½" x 2½"	◣
Unit E–Make 4			
Light	1	3" x 3"	◣
Medium	2	2" x 2"	◣
Unit F–Make 2			
Light	1, 3	2½" x 2½"	◣
Medium	2, 4	2½" x 2½"	◣

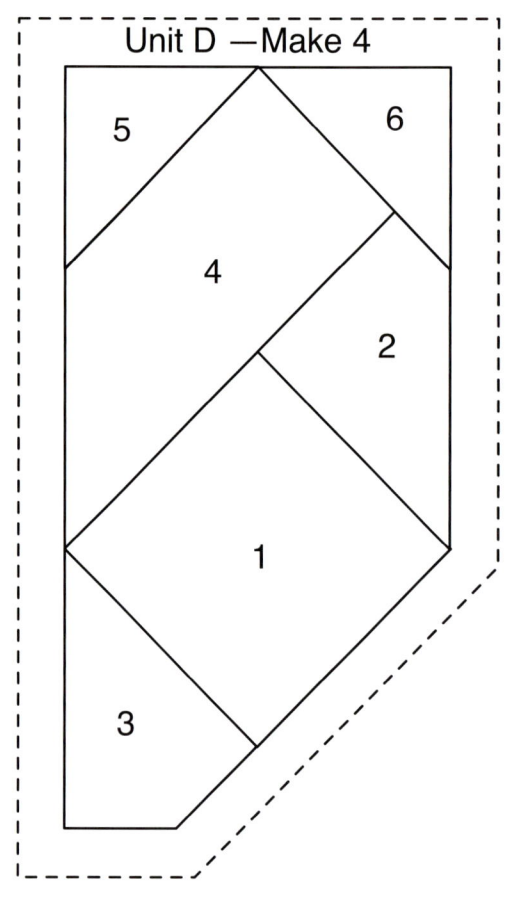

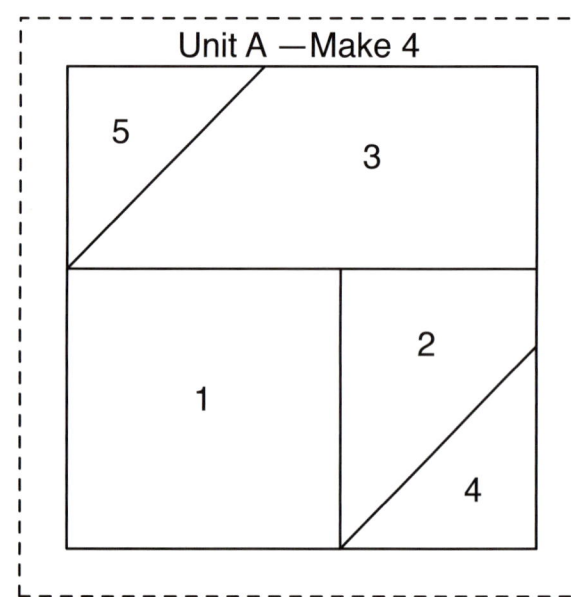

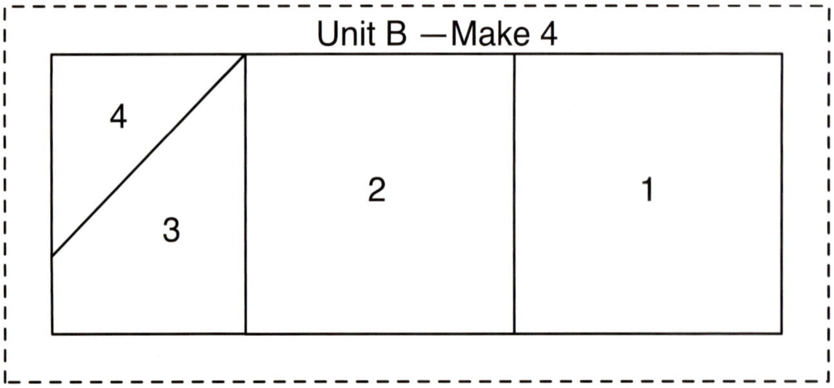

The Broken Branch

NOVEMBER 1935 • 10" BLOCK

CUTTING INSTRUCTIONS

FROM THE BACKGROUND FABRIC, CUT:

1 – 6¾" x 13½" strip. Cut the strip into 2 – 6¾" squares. Cut the squares into half-square triangles.

1 – 2½" x 22½" strip. Cut the strip into 9 – 2½" squares. Cut the squares into half-square triangles. You will have one half-square triangle left over.

FROM THE MEDIUM FABRIC, CUT:

1 – 5½" square. Cut the square into half-square triangles.

1 – 5" square.

1 – 2½" x 25" strip. Cut the strip into 10 – 2½" squares. Cut the squares into half-square triangles. You will have one half-square triangle left over.

FROM THE DARK FABRIC, CUT:

1 – 1½" x 8¼" rectangle.

ASSEMBLING THE BLOCK

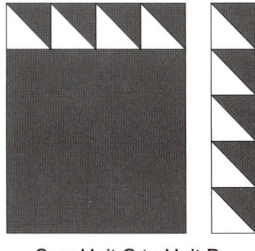

Sew Unit C to Unit D

Sew Unit A to Unit CD

Sew Unit B to Unit E

Assembling instructions continued on page 52.

POSITION CHART

FABRIC	POSITION	SIZE	
Unit A–Make 1			
Medium	1, 3, 5, 7, 9	2½" x 2½"	
Background	2, 4, 6, 8	2½" x 2½"	
Medium	10	5½" x 5½"	
Background	11	6¾" x 6¾"	
Unit B–Make 1			
Medium	1, 3, 5, 7, 9	2½" x 2½"	
Background	2, 4, 6, 8	2½" x 2½"	
Medium	10	5½" x 5½"	
Background	11	6¾" x 6¾"	
Unit C–Make 1			
Background	1, 3, 5, 7, 9	2½" x 2½"	
Medium	2, 4, 6, 8, 10	2½" x 2½"	
Unit D–Make 1			
Medium	1, 3, 5, 7	2½" x 2½"	
Background	2, 4, 6, 8	2½" x 2½"	
Medium	9	5" x 5"	
Unit E–Make 1			
Dark	1	1½" x 8¼"	
Background	2, 3	6¾" x 6¾"	

ASSEMBLING THE BLOCK

Assembling instructions continued from page 51.

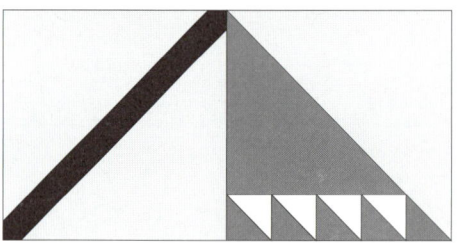

Sew Unit ADC to Unit BE

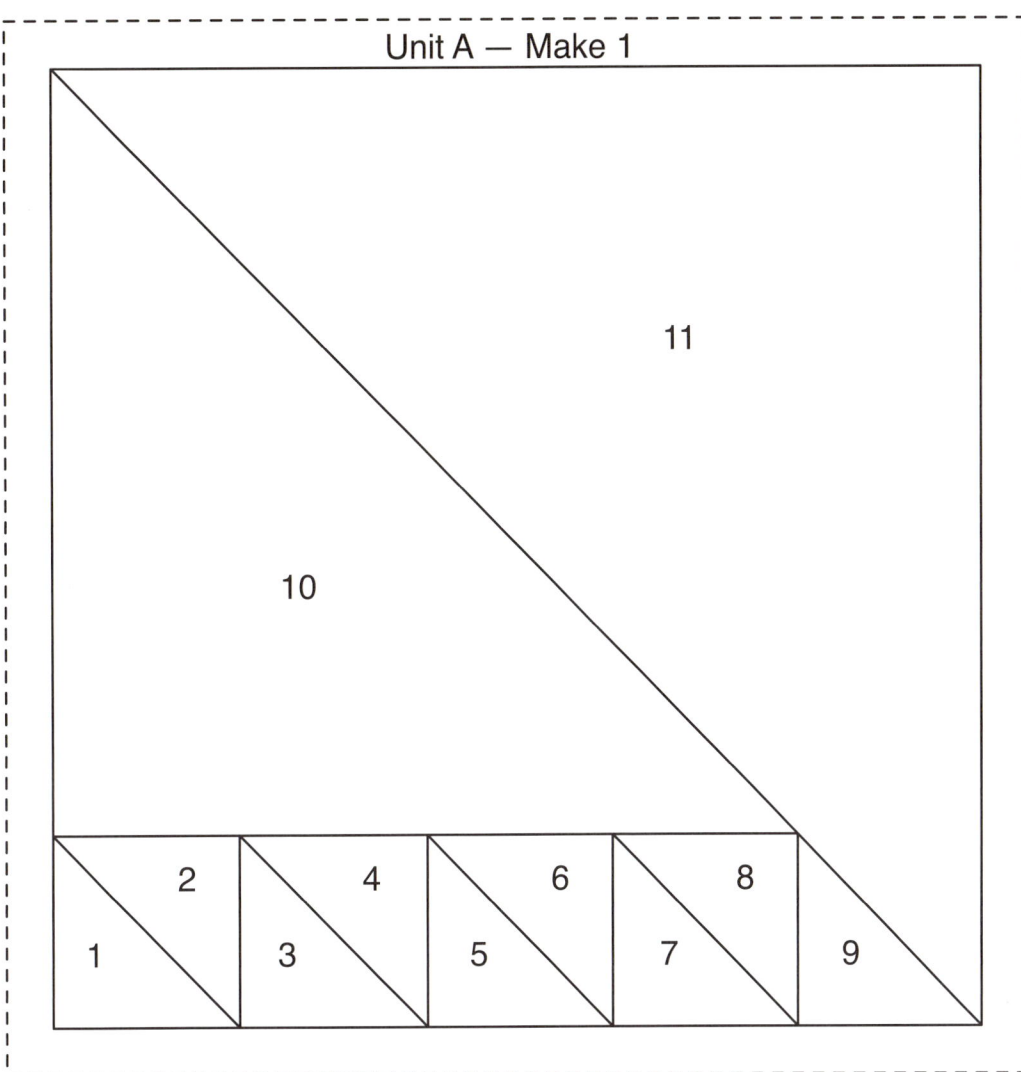

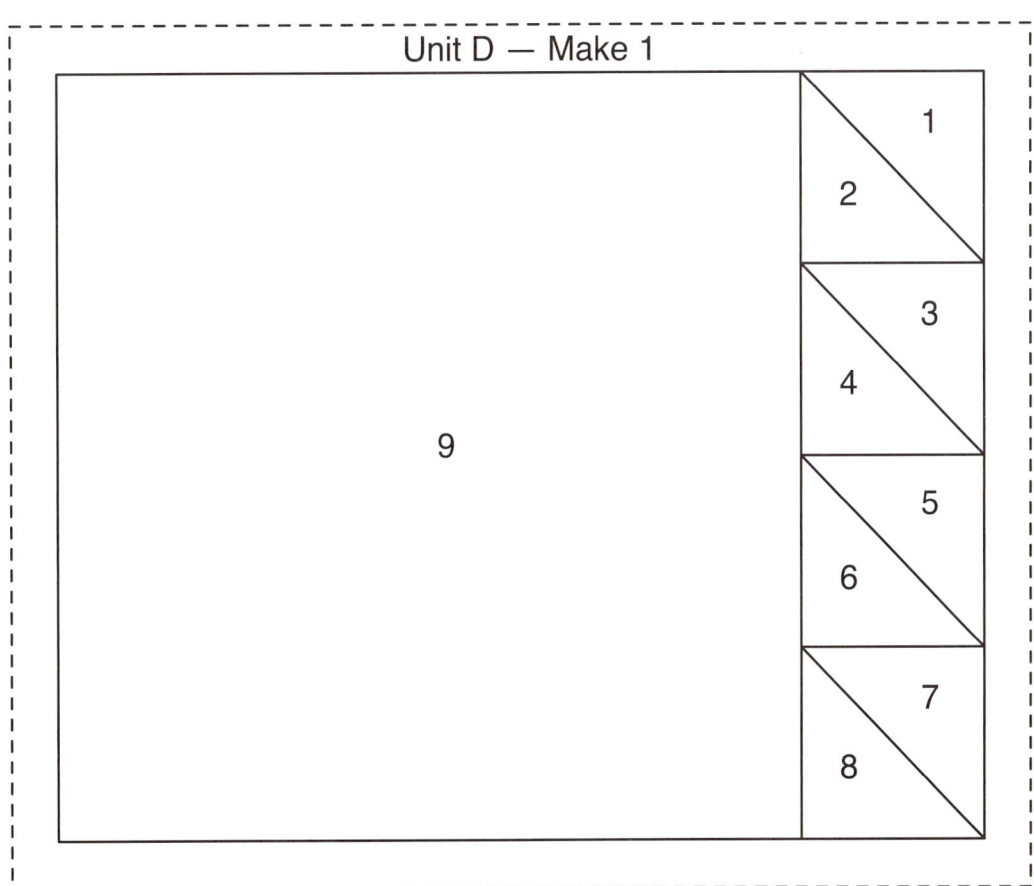

10" THE BROKEN BRANCH | 53

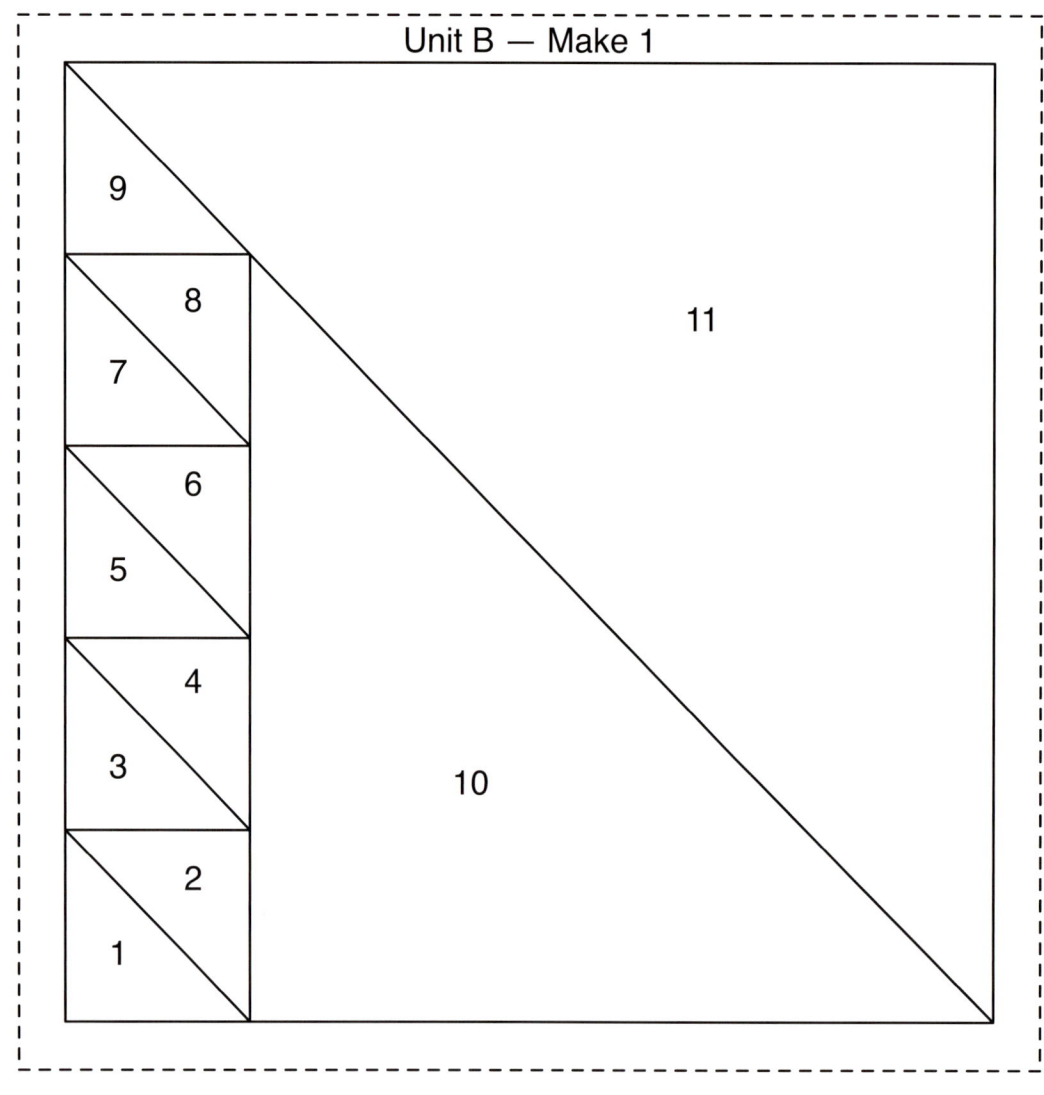

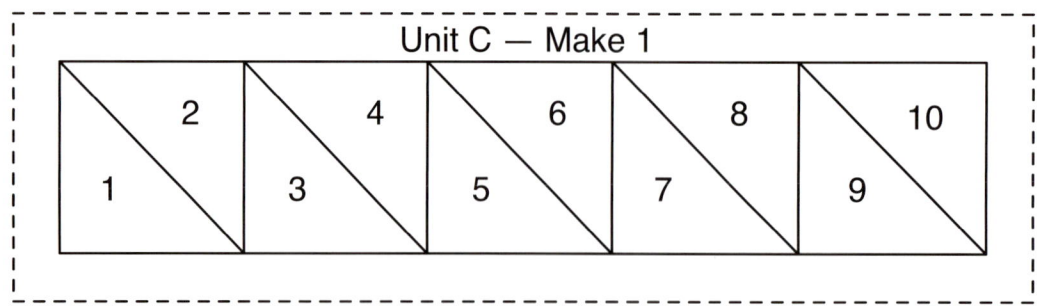

54 | HARD TIMES, SPLENDID QUILTS

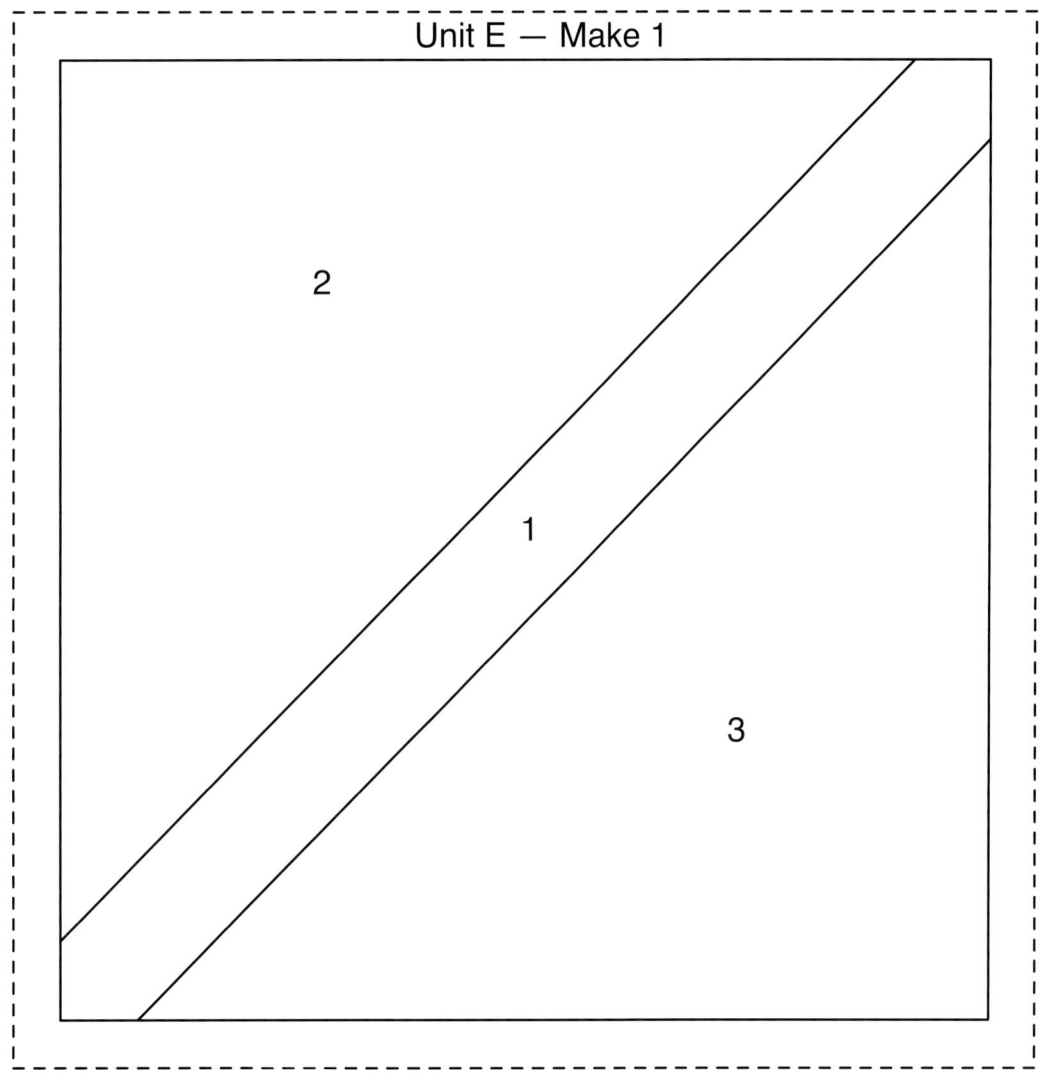

Indian Trail

MAY 1931 • 10" BLOCK

CUTTING INSTRUCTIONS

FROM THE BACKGROUND FABRIC, CUT:

1 – 2¾" x 33" strip. Cut the strip into 12 – 2¾" squares. Cut the squares into half-square triangles.

1 – 2¼" x 9" strip. Cut the strip into 4 – 2¼" squares.

FROM THE LIGHT FABRIC, CUT:

1 – 5¼" x 10½" strip. Cut the strip into 2 – 5¼" squares. Cut the squares into half-square triangles.

FROM THE MEDIUM FABRIC, CUT:

1 – 5¼" x 10½" strip. Cut the strip into 2 – 5¼" squares. Cut the squares into half-square triangles.

FROM THE DARK FABRIC, CUT:

1 – 2¾" x 33" strip. Cut the strip into 12 – 2¾" squares. Cut the squares into half-square triangles.

ASSEMBLING THE BLOCK

Sew each Unit A to a Unit B

Sew two Units AB together as shown

Complete the block as shown

56 | HARD TIMES, SPLENDID QUILTS

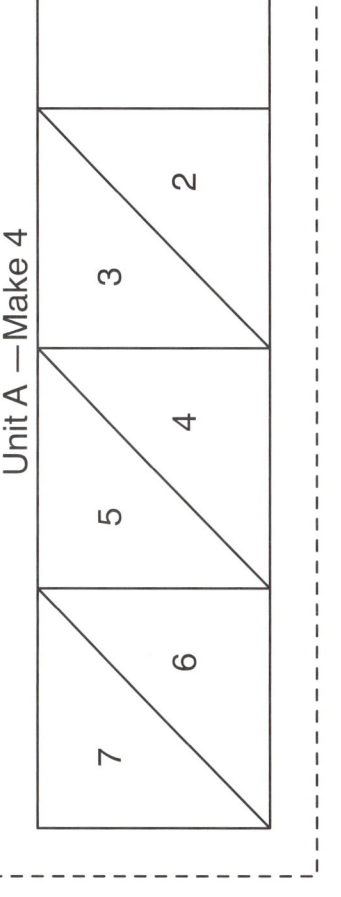

POSITION CHART

FABRIC	POSITION	SIZE	
UNIT A—MAKE 4			
Background	1	2¼" x 2¼"	
Dark	2, 4, 6	2⅝" x 2⅝"	◣
Background	3, 5, 7	2⅝" x 2⅝"	◣
UNIT B—MAKE 4			
Dark	1, 3, 5	2⅝" x 2⅝"	◣
Background	2, 4, 6	2⅝" x 2⅝"	◣
Light	7	5¼" x 5¼"	◣
Medium	8	5¼" x 5¼"	◣

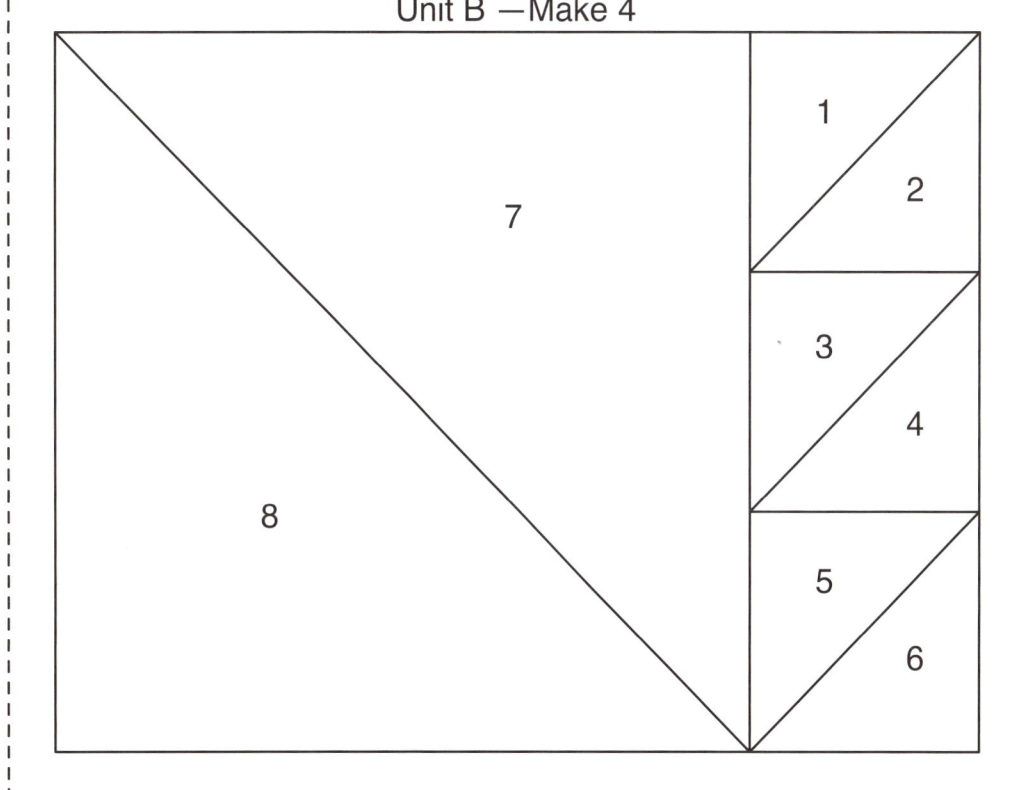

10" INDIAN TRAIL | 57

Railroad Crossing

AUGUST 1935 • 10" BLOCK

CUTTING INSTRUCTIONS

FROM BACKGROUND FABRIC, CUT:

1 – 5½" x 11" strip. Cut the strip into 2 – 5½" squares. Cut the squares into half-square triangles.

1 – 2" x 18" strip. Cut the strip into 4 – 2" x 4½" rectangles.

FROM MEDIUM FABRIC, CUT:

1 – 4½" x 13½" strip. Cut the strip into 3 – 4½" squares. Cut 2 of the squares into half-square triangles.

1 – 2" x 36" strip. Cut the strip into 8 – 2" x 4½" rectangles

ASSEMBLING THE BLOCK

Sew Unit A to Unit B

Sew Units C to Unit AB

POSITION CHART

FABRIC	POSITION	SIZE	
Unit A—Make 1			
Background	1	2" x 4½"	
Medium	2, 3	2" x 4½"	
Medium	4	4½" x 4½"	◣
Medium	5	4½" x 4½"	
Unit B—Make 1			
Background	1	2" x 4½"	
Medium	2, 3	2" x 4½"	
Medium	4	4½" x 4½"	◣
Unit C—Make 2			
Background	1	2" x 4½"	
Medium	2, 3	2" x 4½"	
Background	4, 5	5½" x 5½"	◣
Medium	6	4½" x 4½"	◣

10" RAILROAD CROSSING

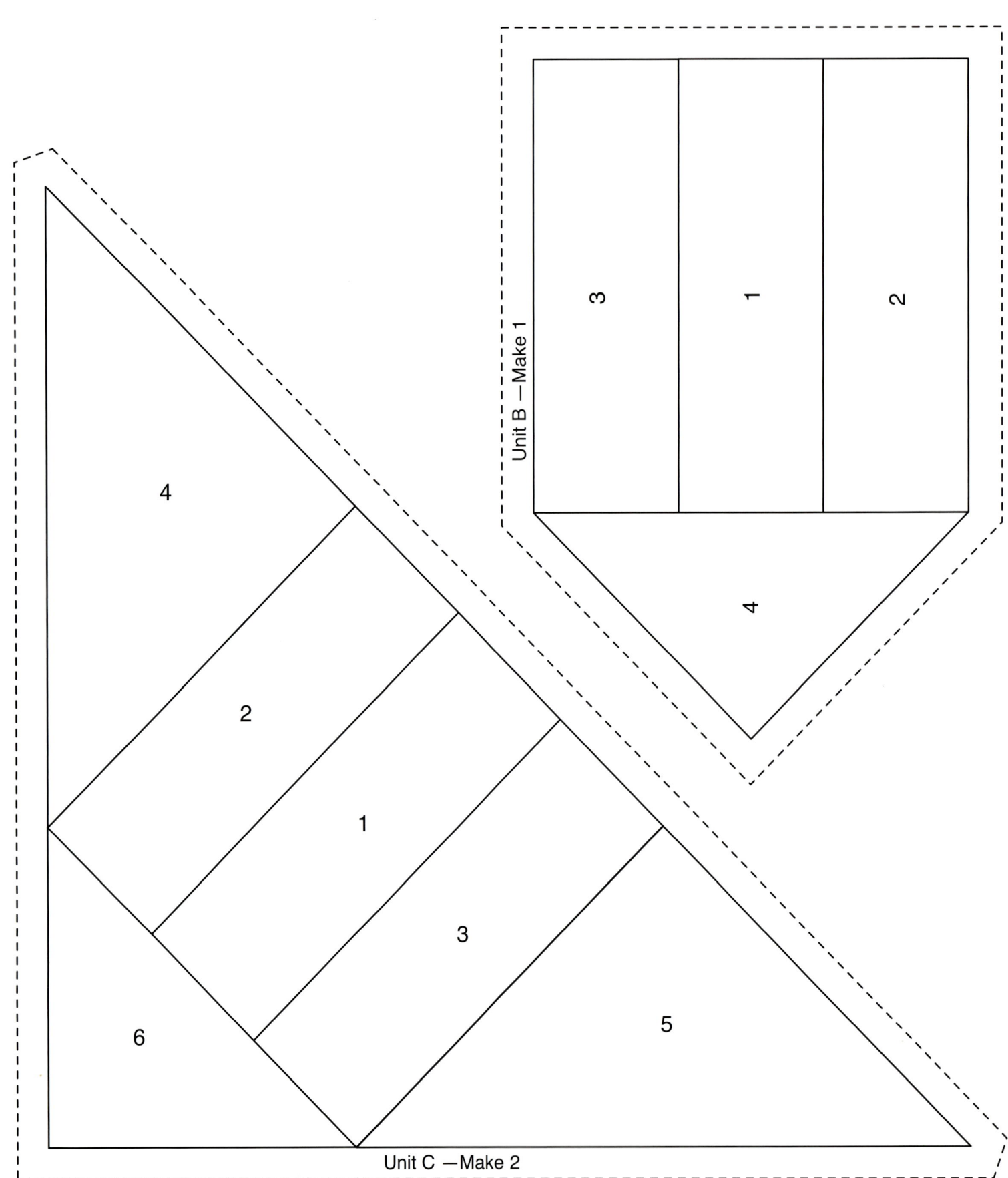

ASSEMBLING THE BLOCK

Continued

Complete the block as shown

POSITION CHART

FABRIC	POSITION	SIZE	
Unit A–Make 4			
Background	1	3" x 3"	◣
Medium	2, 4	1¾" x 3¼"	
Dark	3, 5	1¾" x 3¼"	
Unit B–Make 4			
Dark	1	4¼" x 4¼"	◣
Background	2, 3, 4	4¼" x 4¼"	◣
Unit C–Make 4			
Background	1	3" x 3"	◣
Medium	2, 4	1¾" x 3¼"	
Dark	3	1¾" x 3¼"	
Dark	5	2 ½" x 3½"	

10" WOOD LILY OR INDIAN HEAD

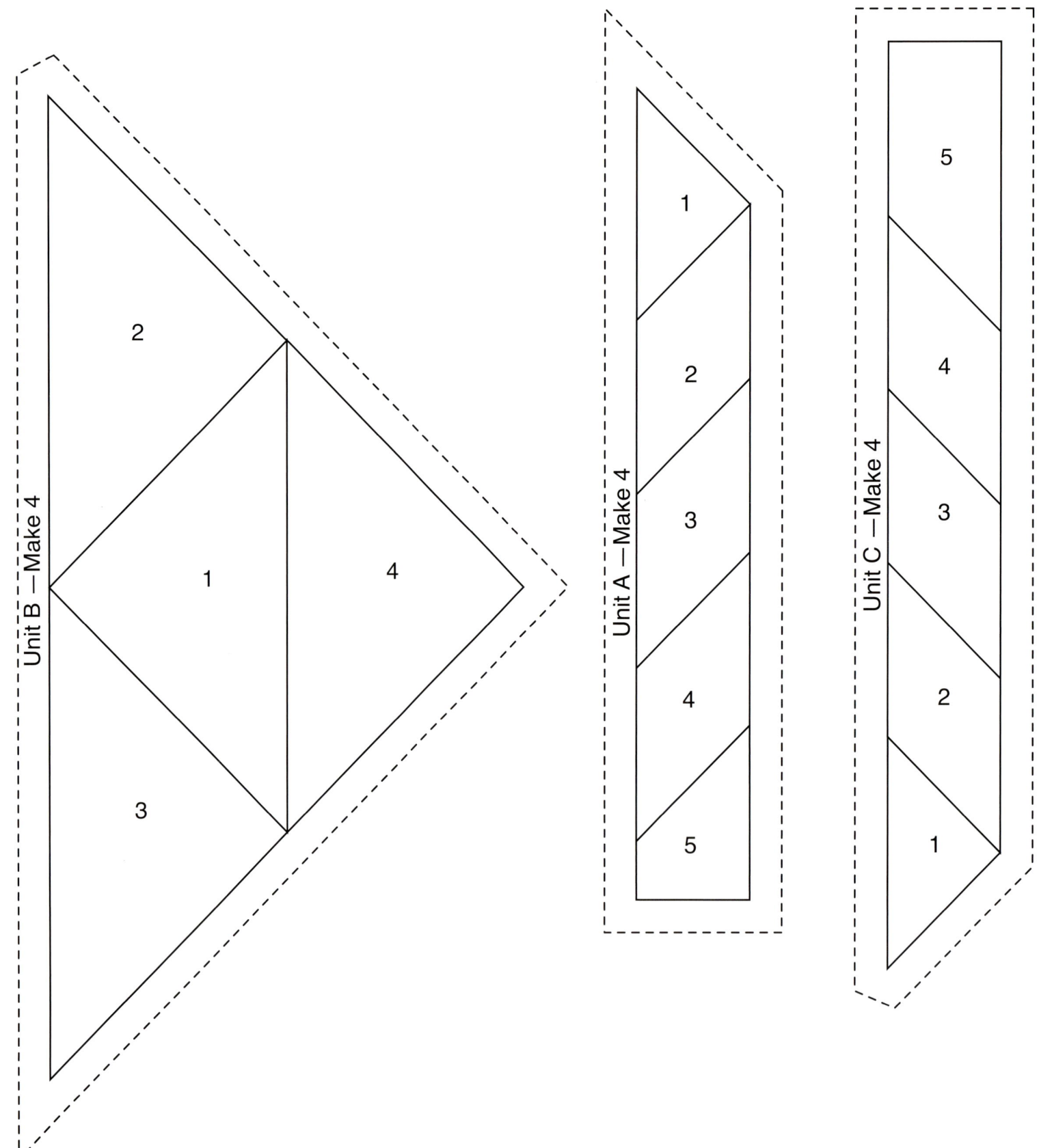

66 | HARD TIMES, SPLENDID QUILTS

Interlocked Squares

SEPTEMBER 1932 • 10" BLOCK

CUTTING INSTRUCTIONS

FROM THE BACKGROUND FABRIC, CUT:

1 – 5¼" x 10½" strip. Cut the strip into 2 – 5¼" squares. Cut the squares into half-square triangles.

1 – 2" x 19" strip. Cut the strip into 4 – 2" x 4¾" rectangles.

1 – 2" x 24" strip. Cut the strip into 4 – 2" x 6" rectangles.

FROM THE MEDIUM FABRIC, CUT:

1 – 4" x 8" strip. Cut the strip into 2 – 4" squares. Cut the squares into half-square triangles.

1 – 2¼" x 4½" strip. Cut the strip into 2 – 2¼" squares. Cut the squares into half-square triangles.

1 – 1¾" x 12" strip. Cut the strip into 4 – 1¾" x 3" rectangles.

FROM THE DARK FABRIC, CUT:

1 – 2¾" x 5½" strip. Cut the strip into 2 – 2¾" squares. Cut the squares into half-square triangles.

1 – 1¾" x 25" strip. Cut the strip into 4 – 1¾" x 6¼" rectangles.

ASSEMBLING THE BLOCK

Sew Units A to Units B

Sew together as shown

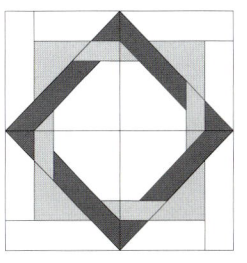

POSITION CHART

FABRIC	POSITION	SIZE	
UNIT A—MAKE 4			
Background	1	5¼" x 5¼"	◩
Medium	2	2¼" x 2¼"	◩
Dark	3	1¾" x 6¼"	
Medium	4	1¾" x 3"	
Dark	5	2¾" x 2¾"	◩
UNIT B—MAKE 4			
Medium	1	4" x 4"	◩
Background	2	2" x 4¾"	
Background	3	2" x 6"	

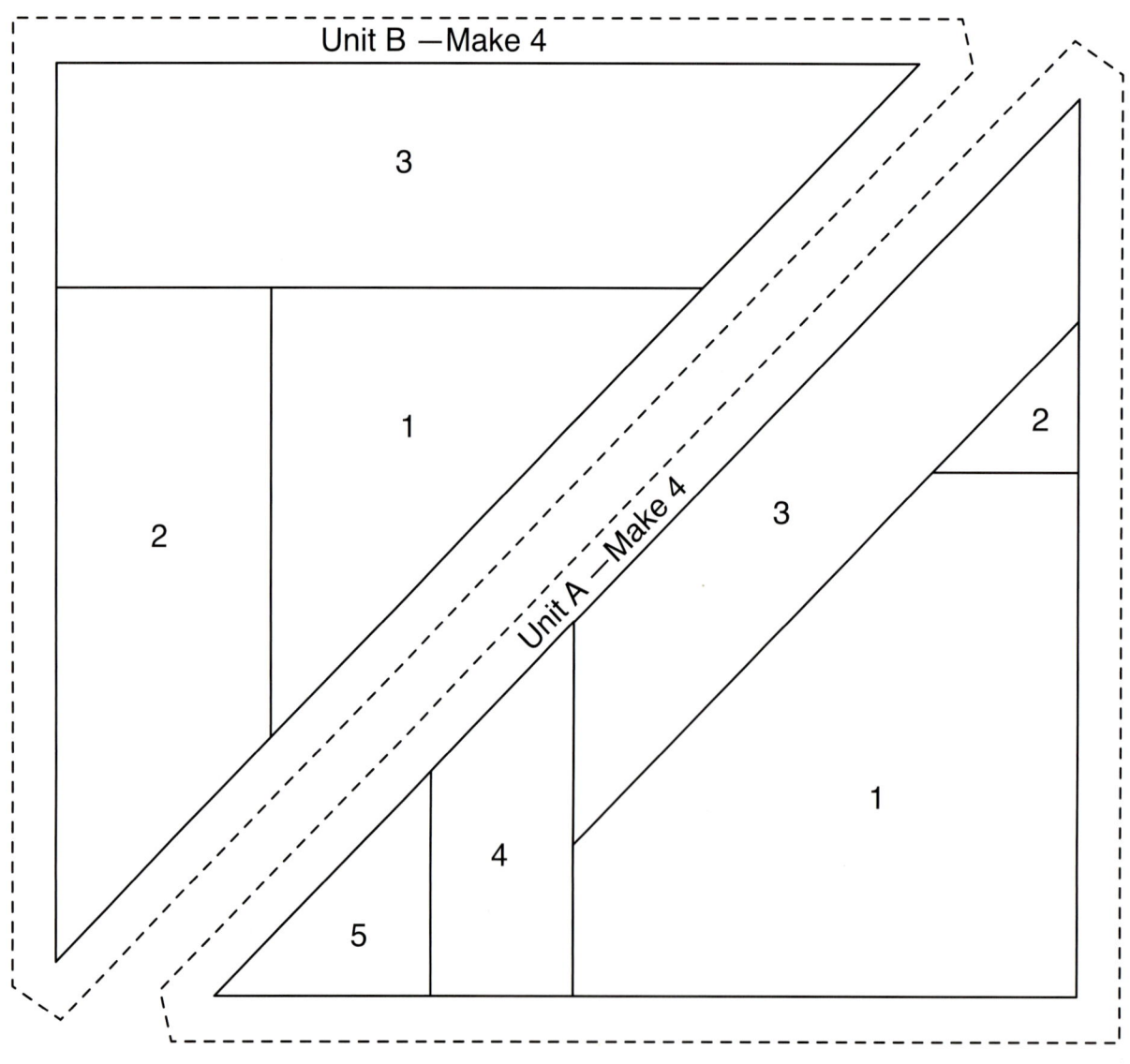

The Star of Bethlehem

APRIL 1937 • 10" BLOCK

CUTTING INSTRUCTIONS

FROM THE BACKGROUND FABRIC, CUT:

1 – 5¼" x 10½" strip. Cut the strip into 2 – 5¼" squares. Cut the squares into half-square triangles.

1 – 3½" x 14" strip. Cut the strip into 4 – 3½" squares.

1 – 1¾" x 21" strip. Cut the strip into 2 – 1¾" x 4½" rectangles and 2 – 1¾" x 6" rectangles.

FROM THE MEDIUM FABRIC, CUT:

1 – 4½" square.

1 – 4" x 16" strip. Cut the strip into 4 – 4" squares. Cut the squares into half-square triangles.

ASSEMBLING THE BLOCK

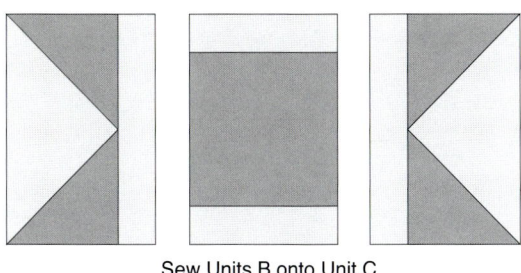

Sew Units B onto Unit C

Sew Units A onto Unit BC

POSITION CHART

FABRIC	POSITION	SIZE
Unit A–Make 2		
Background	1	5¼" x 5¼"
Medium	2, 3	4" x 4"
Background	4, 5	3½" x 3½"
Unit B–Make 2		
Background	1	5¼" x 5¼"
Medium	2, 3	4" x 4"
Background	4	1¾" x 6"
Unit C–Make 1		
Medium	1	4½" x 4½"
Background	2, 3	1¾" x 4½"

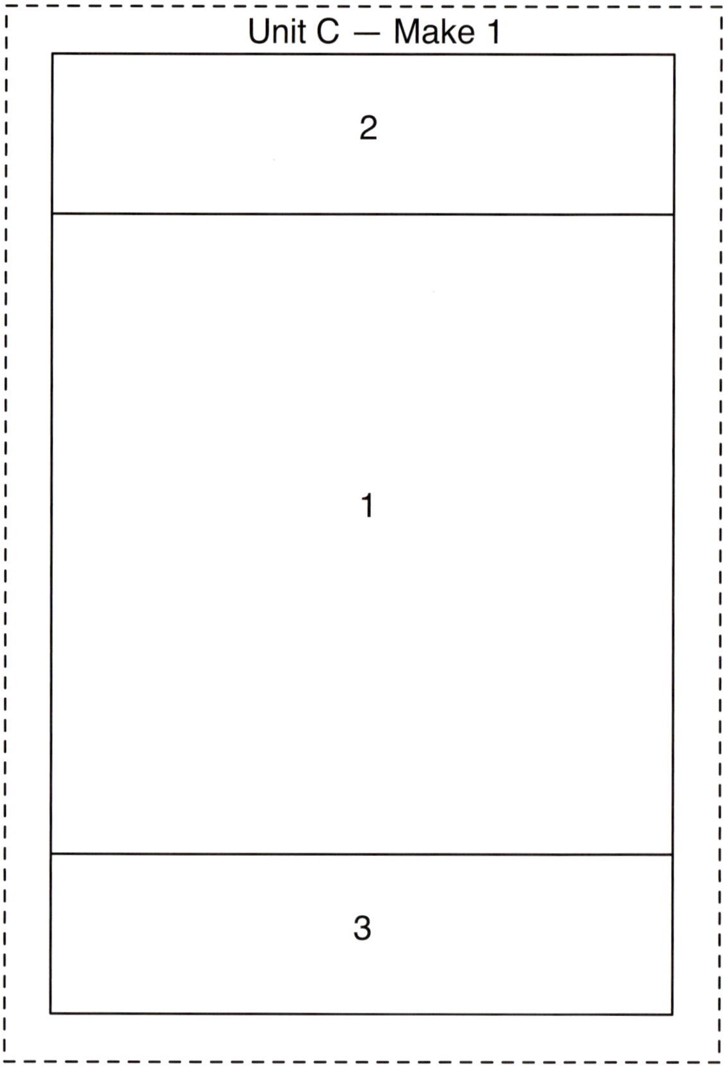

Unit C — Make 1

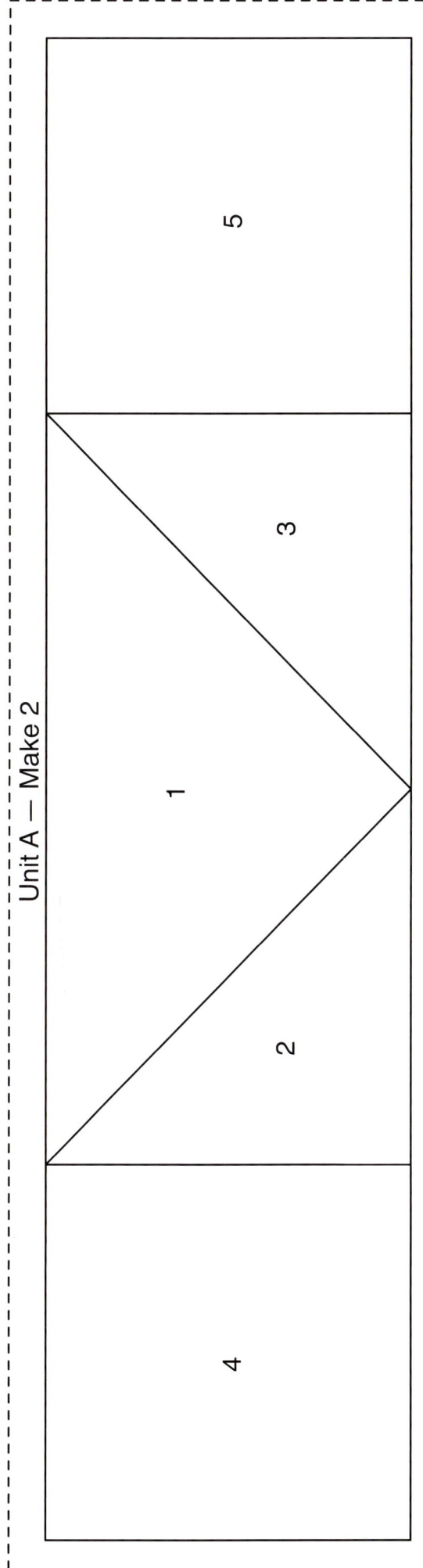
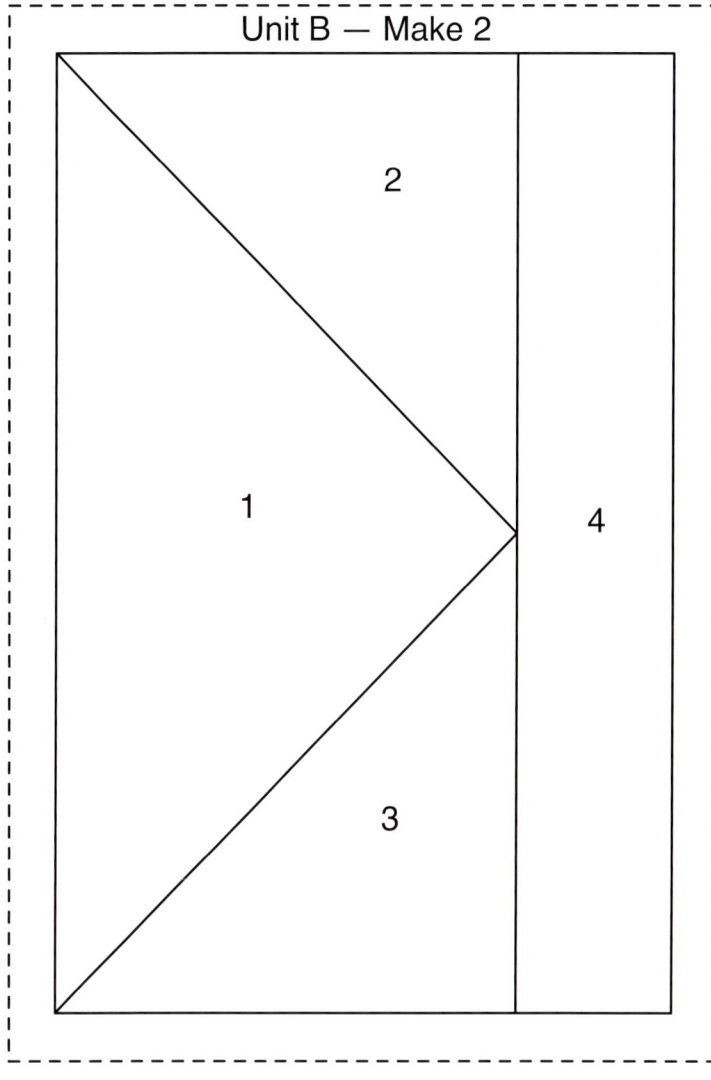

10" THE STAR OF BETHLEHEM | 71

1930s Sampler Quilt

FINISHING INSTRUCTIONS

TO MAKE THE QUILT

Make 20 blocks using fabrics of your choice.

Sashing: Cut 17 strips 2½" across the width of the fabric. Cut into 49 – 2½" x 10½" rectangles.

Corner Stones: Cut 30 – 2½" squares from various fabrics.

Sew a sashing strip between the blocks. Sew the blocks together in rows. Sew the corner stones onto sashing strips, making a long strip for the top and bottom of the block rows. Sew the rows together alternating sashing/corner stone strip with strips of blocks.

Layer the quilt with batting and backing. Quilt. Cut 6 – 2½" strips the width of the fabric for the binding.

Hard Times made by Carolyn Cullinan McCormick, Franktown, Colorado, quilted by Tracy Peterson Yadon, Lady Quilter, Manhattan, Montana.

This miniature quilt was made and quilted by Carolyn Cullinan McCormick, Franktown, Colorado. Bethlehem Stars are surrounded by one inch strips of reproduction fabric and set on point.

A Gallery of Ideas

Are you wondering what to make using these paper pieced patterns? Step into our gallery and gather a few ideas.

Diane Donnelly of Bozeman, Montana, stitched together four Chisolm Trail blocks and put them on point to make this striking wallhanging. It was quilted by Tracy Peterson Yadon, Lady Quilter, Manhattan, Montana.

GALLERY | 73

Above: Marie Huber of Glendive, Montana, made this 10" sampler. It was quilted by Common Threads Custom Quilting of Glendive, Montana.
Right: This sampler, using 4" blocks, was made by Marilyn Vap, Ginny Rafferty, Julie Lilly, Jackie Parker, Kathy Safer, Polly Somers, Brenda Williams, Carol Bonetti, Romona Hamline, Carol Neely, Diane Varner, Patrice Heath and Donna Thalimer.

Above: This Grandmother's Favorite quilt was made by Carolyn Cullinan McCormick, Franktown, Colorado, and quilted by Tracy Peterson Yadon, Lady Quilter, Manhattan, Montana. **Below:** This 1938 Basket quilt was made by Carolyn Cullinan McCormick, Franktown, Colorado and quilted by Tracy Peterson Yadon, Lady Quilter, Manhattan, Montana.

Megan McCormick of Denver, Colorado, made this enchanting sampler using the 10" patterns. The quilt was quilted by Tracy Peterson Yadon, Lady Quilter, Manhattan, Montana.

Above: Montana Stampede made and quilted by Debbie Dent of Wilsall, Montana.

Above: Here's a cheerful six-block wall hanging made and quilted by Carolyn Cullinan McCormick, Franktown, Colorado. **Left:** This wallhanging, Seasonal Symbols, was made by Carol Netwal of Castle Rock, Colorado, and was quilted by Tracy Peterson Yadon, Lady Quilter, Manhattan, Montana.

Above: This lovely table runner was made using two 10" Lone Star of Paradise blocks set on point. It was pieced and quilted by Carolyn Cullinan McCormick, Franktown, Colorado.

76 | HARD TIMES, SPLENDID QUILTS

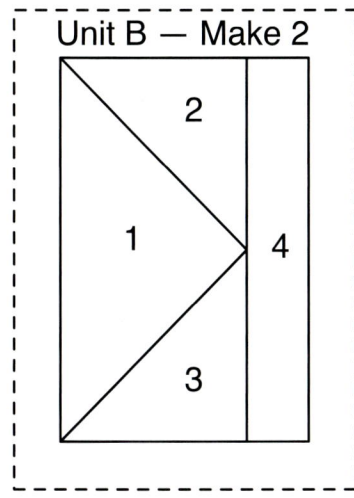

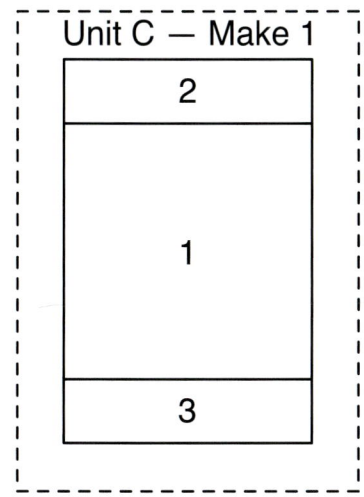

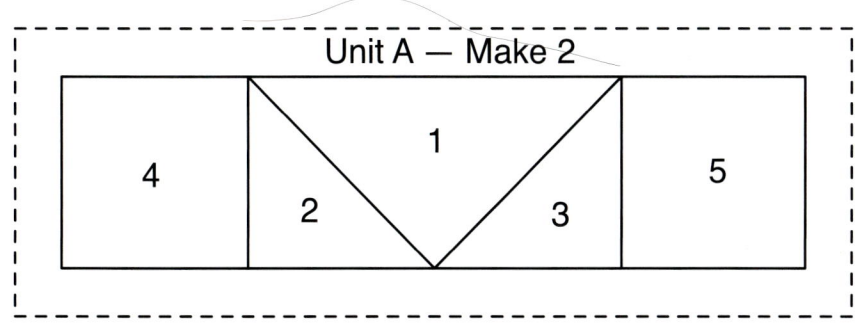

POSITION CHART

FABRIC	POSITION	SIZE
Unit A–Make 2		
Background	1	2¾" x 2¾"
Medium	2, 3	2" x 2"
Background	4, 5	1¾" x 1¾"
Unit B–Make 2		
Background	1	2¾" x 2¾"
Medium	2, 3	2" x 2"
Background	4	1" x 3"
Unit C–Make 1		
Medium	1	2¼" x 2¼"
Background	2, 3	1" x 2¼"

The Broken Branch

NOVEMBER 1935 • 4" BLOCK

CUTTING INSTRUCTIONS

FROM THE BACKGROUND FABRIC, CUT:

1 – 3¼" x 6½" strip. Cut the strip into 2 – 3¼" squares. Cut the squares into half-square triangles.

1 – 1½" x 13½" strip. Cut the strip into 9 – 1½" squares. Cut the squares into half-square triangles. You will have one half-square triangle left over.

FROM THE MEDIUM FABRIC, CUT:

1 – 2⅜" square. Cut the square into half-square triangles.

1 – 2½" square.

1 – 1½" x 15" strip. Cut the strip into 10 – 1½" squares. Cut the squares into half-square triangles. You will have 1 half-square triangle left over.

FROM THE DARK FABRIC, CUT:

1 – ¾" x 4¼" rectangle.

ASSEMBLING THE BLOCK

Sew Unit C to Unit D

Sew Unit A to Unit CD

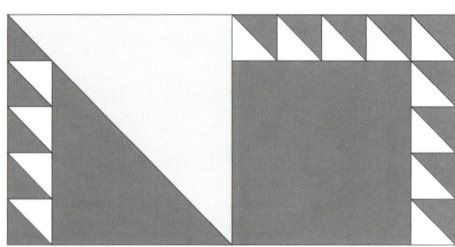

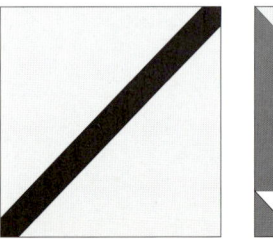

Sew Unit B to Unit E

Sew Unit ADC to Unit BE

86 | HARD TIMES, SPLENDID QUILTS

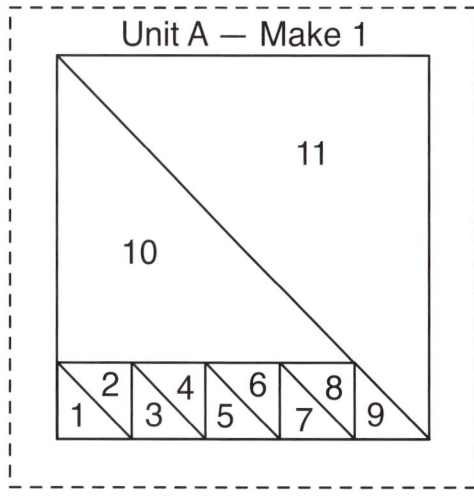

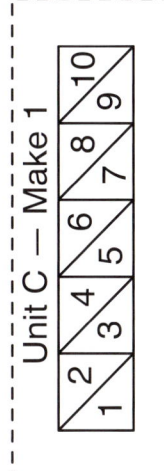

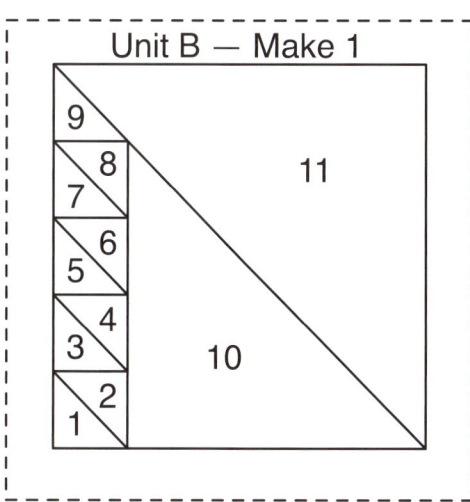

POSITION CHART

FABRIC	POSITION	SIZE	
Unit A-Make 1			
Medium	1, 3, 5, 7, 9	1½" x 1½"	◣
Background	2, 4, 6, 8	1½" x 1½"	◣
Medium	10	2¾" x 2¾"	◣
Background	11	3¼" x 3¼"	◣
Unit B-Make 1			
Medium	1, 3, 5, 7, 9	1½" x 1½"	◣
Background	2, 4, 6, 8	1½" x 1½"	◣
Medium	10	2¾" x 2¾"	◣
Background	11	3¼" x 3¼"	◣
Unit C-Make 1			
Background	1, 3, 5, 7, 9	1½" x 1½"	◣
Medium	2, 4, 6, 8, 10	1½" x 1½"	◣
Unit D-Make 1			
Medium	1, 3, 5, 7	1½" x 1½"	◣
Background	2, 4, 6, 8	1½" x 1½"	◣
Medium	9	2½" x 2½"	
Unit E-Make 1			
Dark	1	¾" x 4¼"	
Background	2, 3	3¼" x 3¼"	◣

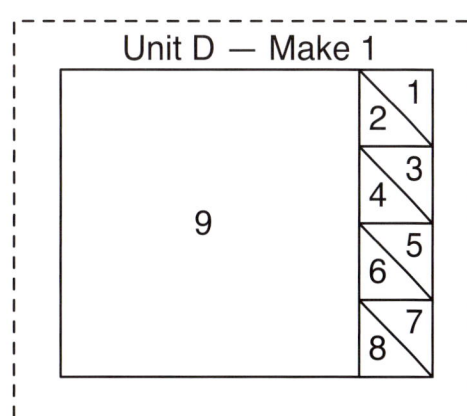

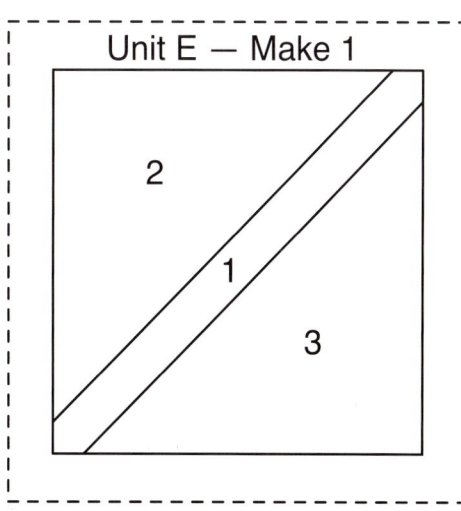

4" BLOCK OR PROJECT NAME | 87

Solomon's Temple

NOVEMBER 1936 • 4" BLOCK

CUTTING INSTRUCTIONS

FROM THE BACKGROUND FABRIC, CUT:

1 – 2¾" x 5½" strip. Cut the strip into 2 – 2¾" squares. Cut the squares into half-square triangles.

1 – 1½" x 36" strip. Cut the strip into 24 – 1½" squares. Cut eighteen squares into half-square triangles.

FROM THE MEDIUM FABRIC, CUT:

1 – 2½" x 5" strip. Cut the strip into 2 – 2½" squares. Cut the squares into half-square triangles.

1 – 2" square.

1 – 1½" x 36" strip. Cut the strips into 24 – 1½" squares. Cut 22 squares into half-square triangles.

ASSEMBLING THE BLOCK

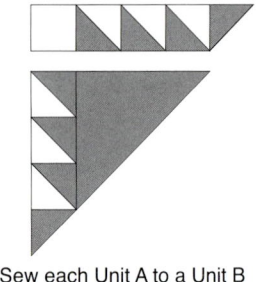

Sew each Unit A to a Unit B

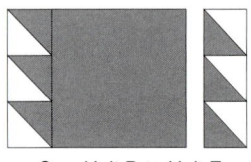

Sew Unit D to Unit E

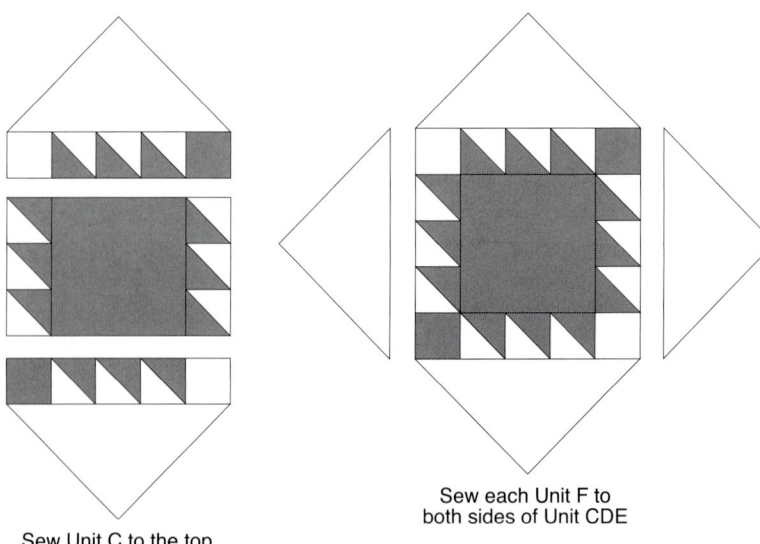

Sew Unit C to the top and bottom of Unit DE

Sew each Unit F to both sides of Unit CDE

88 | HARD TIMES, SPLENDID QUILTS

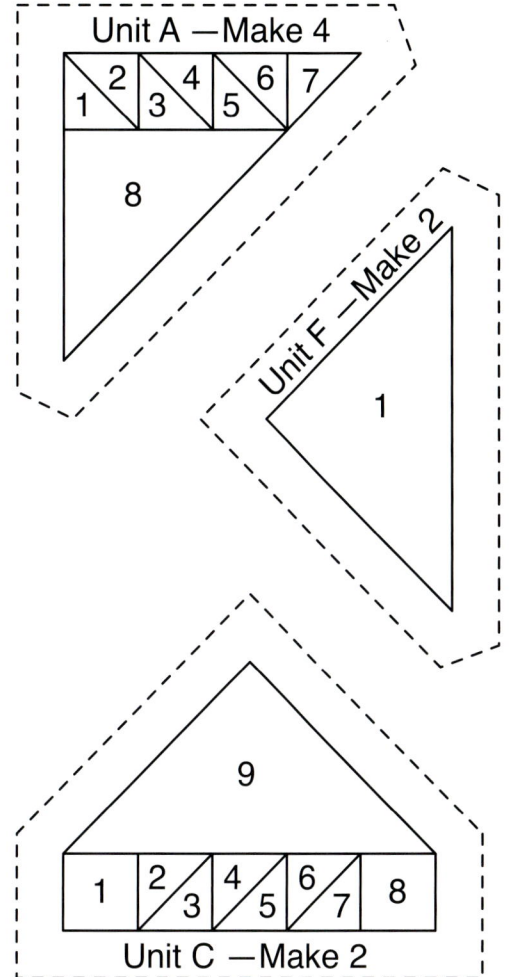
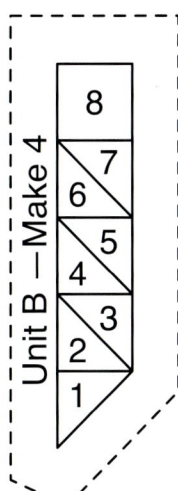
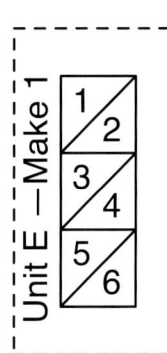

POSITION CHART

FABRIC	POSITION	SIZE	
Unit A–Make 4			
Medium	1, 3, 5, 7	1½" x 1½"	◼
Background	2, 4, 6	1½" x 1½"	◼
Medium	8	2½" x 2½"	◼
Unit B–Make 4			
Medium	1, 3, 5, 7	1½" x 1½"	◼
Background	2, 4, 6	1½" x 1½"	◼
Background	8	1½" x 1½"	
Unit C–Make 2			
Medium	1	1½" x 1½"	
Background	2, 4, 6	1½" x 1½"	◼
Medium	3, 5, 7	1½" x 1½"	◼
Background	8	1½" x 1½"	
Background	9	2¾" x 2¾"	◼
Unit D–Make 1			
Background	1, 3, 5	1½" x 1½"	◼
Medium	2, 4, 6	1½" x 1½"	◼
Medium	7	2" x 2"	
Unit E–Make 1			
Medium	1, 3, 5	1½" x 1½"	◼
Background	2, 4, 6	1½" x 1½"	◼
Unit F–Make 2			
Background	1	2¾" x 2¾"	◼

Sew each AB Unit to Unit CDEF

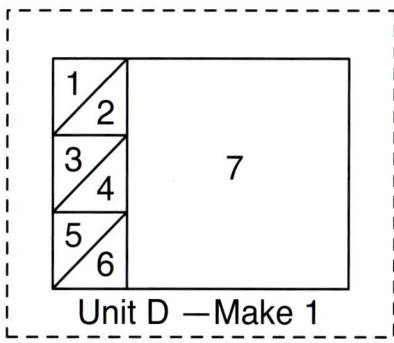

4" SOLOMON'S TEMPLE | 89

Feathered Edge Star

1934 • 4" BLOCK

CUTTING INSTRUCTIONS

FROM THE BACKGROUND FABRIC, CUT:

1 – 2¼" x 13½" strip. Cut the strip into 6 – 2¼" squares. Cut 2 of the squares into half-square triangles.

1 – 1¼" x 37½" strip. Cut the strip into 30 – 1¼" squares. Cut the squares into half-square triangles.

FROM THE MEDIUM FABRIC, CUT:

1 – 1¾" x 3½" strip. Cut the strip into 2 – 1¾" squares. Cut the squares into half-square triangles.

1 – 1¼" x 25" strip. Cut the strip into 20 – 1¼" squares. Cut the squares into half-square triangles.

1 – 1" x 18" strip. Cut the strip into 8 – 1" x 1¼" rectangles and 8 – 1" x 1" squares.

FROM THE DARK FABRIC, CUT:

1 – 1¾" x 8¾" strip. Cut the strip into 5 – 1¾" squares. Cut 4 of the squares into half-square triangles.

ASSEMBLING THE BLOCK

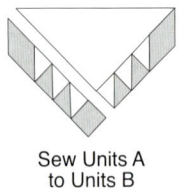
Sew Units A to Units B

Sew Units AB to Units C

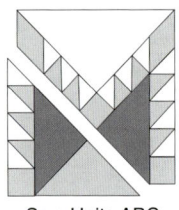
Sew Units ABC to Units D

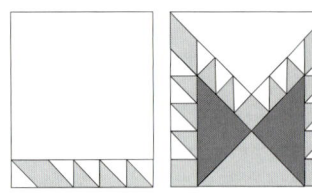
Sew Units ABCD to Units E

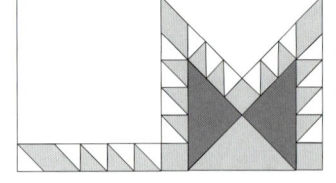
Sew Units ABCDE to Units F

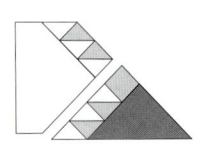
Sew Units G to Units H

Sew Units GH to Unit I

Sew together as shown

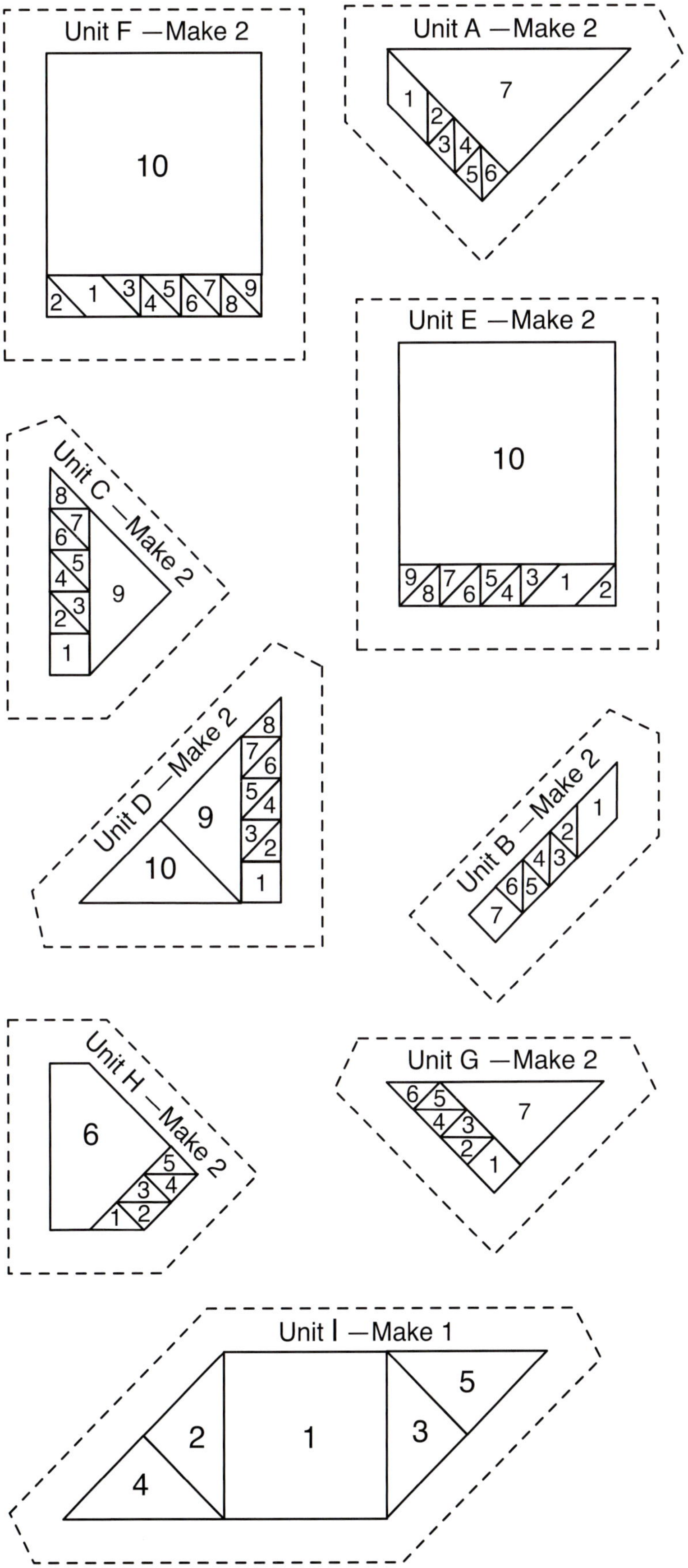

POSITION CHART

Unit A–Make 2
Fabric	Position	Size
Medium	1	1" x 1¼"
Background	2, 4, 6	1¼" x 1¼" ◣
Medium	3, 5	1¼" x 1¼" ◣
Background	7	2¼" x 2¼" ◣

Unit B–Make 2
Fabric	Position	Size
Medium	1	1" x 1¼"
Background	2, 4, 6	1¼" x 1¼" ◣
Medium	3, 5	1¼" x 1¼" ◣
Medium	7	1" x 1"

Unit C–Make 2
Fabric	Position	Size
Medium	1	1" x 1"
Background	2, 4, 6, 8	1¼" x 1¼" ◣
Medium	3, 5, 7	1¼" x 1¼" ◣
Dark	9	1¾" x 1¾" ◣

Unit D–Make 2
Fabric	Position	Size
Medium	1	1" x 1"
Background	2, 4, 6, 8	1¼" x 1¼" ◣
Medium	3, 5, 7	1¼" x 1¼" ◣
Dark	9	1¾" x 1¾" ◣
Medium	10	1¾" x 1¾" ◣

Unit E and F–Make 2 of each
Fabric	Position	Size
Medium	1	1" x 1¼"
Background	2, 3, 5, 7, 9	1¼" x 1¼" ◣
Medium	4, 6, 8	1¼" x 1¼" ◣
Background	10	2¼" x 2¼"

Unit G–Make 2
Fabric	Position	Size
Medium	1	1" x 1"
Background	2, 4, 6	1¼" x 1¼" ◣
Medium	3, 5	1¼" x 1¼" ◣
Dark	7	1¾" x 1¾" ◣

Unit H–Make 2
Fabric	Position	Size
Background	1, 3, 5	1¼" x 1¼" ◣
Medium	2, 4	1¼" x 1¼"
Background	6	2¼" x 2¼" ◣

Unit I–Make 1
Fabric	Position	Size
Dark	1	1¾" x 1¾"
Medium	2, 3	1¾" x 1¾" ◣
Dark	4, 5	1¾" x 1¾" ◣

4" FEATHERED EDGE STAR

The Ladies Aid Album

JANUARY 1938 • 4" BLOCK

CUTTING INSTRUCTIONS

FROM THE BACKGROUND FABRIC, CUT:

1 – 2¼" x 3½" rectangle.

1 – 1¼" x 9" strip. Cut the strip into 4 – 1¼" x 2¼" rectangles.

FROM THE MEDIUM FABRIC, CUT:

1 – 2¼" x 9" strip. Cut the strip into 4 – 2¼" squares

1 – 2" square. Cut the square into half-square triangles.

FROM THE DARK FABRIC, CUT:

1 – 2" x 8" strip. Cut the strip into 4 – 2" squares. Cut the squares into half-square triangles.

ASSEMBLING THE BLOCK

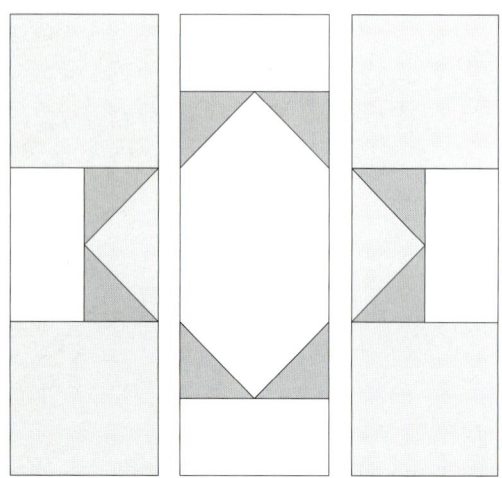

Sew each Unit B to Unit A

92 | HARD TIMES, SPLENDID QUILTS

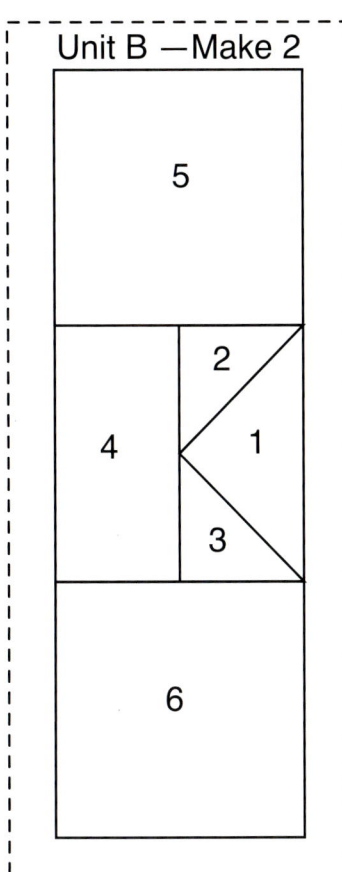

POSITION CHART

FABRIC	POSITION	SIZE	
Unit A-Make 1			
Background	1	2¼" x 3½"	
Dark	2, 3, 4, 5	2" x 2"	◣
Background	6, 7	1¼" x 2¼"	
Unit B-Make 2			
Medium	1	2" x 2"	◣
Dark	2, 3	2" x 2"	◣
Background	4	1¼" x 2¼"	
Medium	5, 6	2¼" x 2¼"	

4" LADIES AID ALBUM | 93

The Kite

JANUARY 1937 • 4" BLOCK

CUTTING INSTRUCTIONS

FROM THE BACKGROUND FABRIC, CUT:

1 – 2¾" x 5½" strip. Cut the strip into 2 – 2¾" squares. Cut the squares into half-square triangles.

1 – 1½" x 6" strip. Cut the strip into 4 – 1½" squares. Cut the squares into half-square triangles.

1 – 1¼" x 23" strip. Cut the strip into 8 – 1¼" x 1¾" rectangles and 4 – 1¼" x 2¼" rectangles.

FROM THE MEDIUM FABRIC, CUT:

1 – 1¾" x 9" strip. Cut the strip into 4 – 1¾" x 2¼" rectangles.

1 – 1¼" x 24" strip. Cut the strip into 16 – 1¼" x 1½" rectangles.

FROM THE DARK FABRIC, CUT:

1 – 1½" x 11" strip. Cut the strip into 4 – 1½" x 2¾" rectangles.

ASSEMBLING THE BLOCK

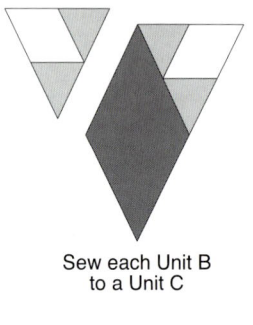

Sew each Unit B to a Unit C

Sew each Unit D to a Unit BC

Sew each Unit A to a Unit BCD

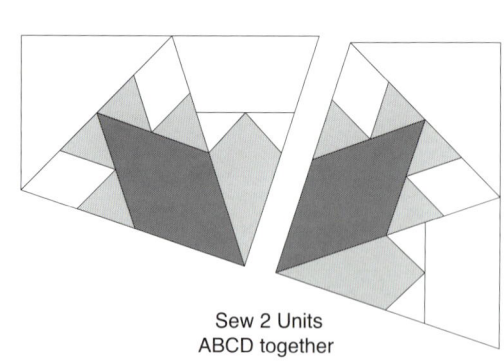

Sew 2 Units ABCD together

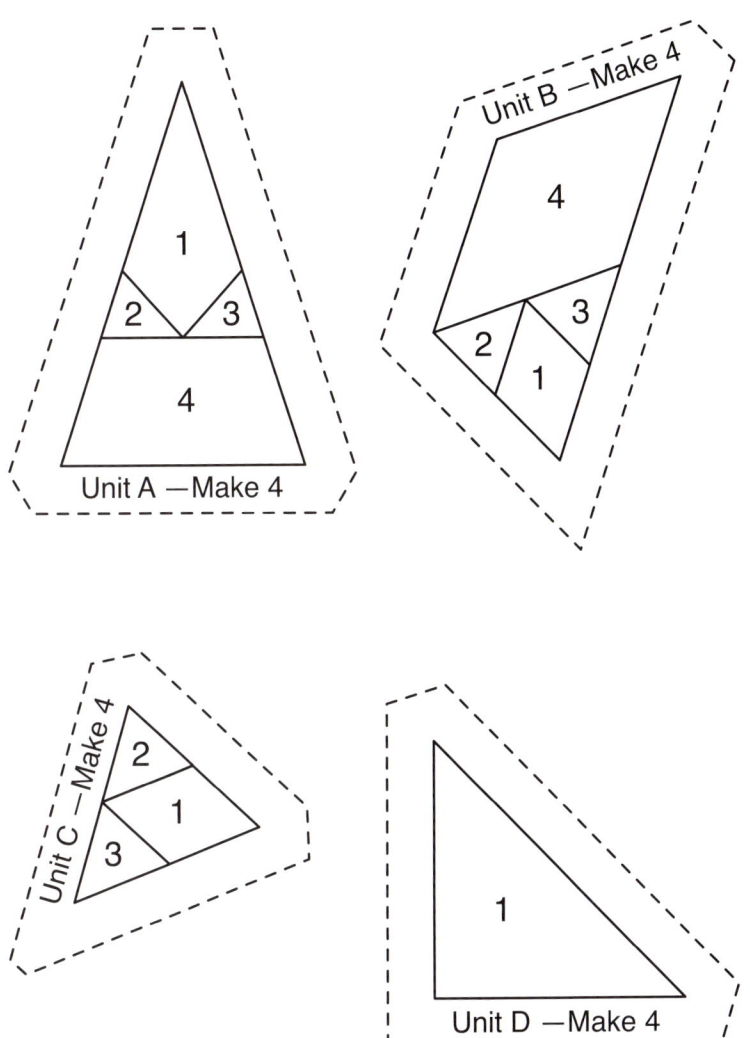

POSITION CHART

FABRIC	POSITION	SIZE
Unit A-Make 4		
Medium	1	1¾" x 2¼"
Background	2, 3	1½" x 1½" ◣
Background	4	1¼" x 2¼"
Unit B-Make 4		
Background	1	1¼" x 1¾"
Medium	2, 3	1¼" x 1½"
Dark	4	1½" x 2¾"
Unit C-Make 4		
Background	1	1¼" x 1¾"
Medium	2, 3	1¼" x 1½"
Unit D-Make 4		
Background	1	2¾" x 2¾" ◣

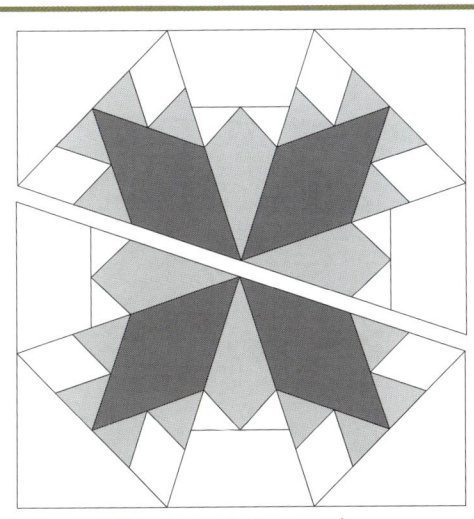

Sew the two halves together to complete the block.

Indian Trail

MAY 1931 • 4" BLOCK

CUTTING INSTRUCTIONS

FROM THE BACKGROUND FABRIC, CUT:

1 – 1½" x 18" strip. Cut the strip into 12 – 1½" squares. Cut the squares into half-square triangles.

1 – 1¼" x 5" strip. Cut the strip into 4 – 1¼" squares.

FROM THE LIGHT FABRIC, CUT:

1 – 2¾" x 5½" strip. Cut the strip into 2 – 2¾" squares. Cut the squares into half-square triangles.

FROM THE MEDIUM FABRIC, CUT:

1 – 2¾" x 5½" strip. Cut the strip into 2 – 2¾" squares. Cut the squares into half-square triangles.

FROM THE DARK FABRIC, CUT:

1 – 1½" x 18" strip. Cut the strip into 12 – 1½" squares. Cut the squares into half-square triangles.

ASSEMBLING THE BLOCK

Sew each Unit A to a Unit B

Sew two Units AB together as shown

Complete the block as shown

96 | HARD TIMES, SPLENDID QUILTS

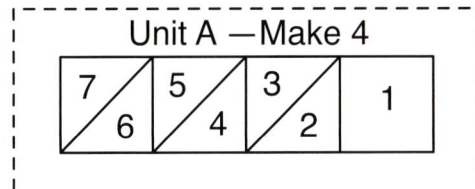

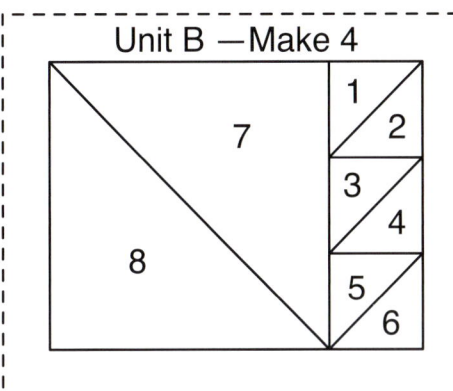

POSITION CHART

FABRIC	POSITION	SIZE
Unit A–Make 4		
Background	1	1¼" x 1¼"
Dark	2, 4, 6	1½" x 1½"
Background	3, 5, 7	1½" x 1½"
Unit B–Make 4		
Dark	1, 3, 5	1½" x 1½"
Background	2, 4, 6	1½" x 1½"
Light	7	2¾" x 2¾"
Medium	8	2¾" x 2¾"

4" INDIAN TRAIL | 97

The Lone Star of Paradise

MARCH 1933 • 4" BLOCK

CUTTING INSTRUCTIONS

FROM THE BACKGROUND FABRIC, CUT:

1 – 1½" x 24" strip. Cut the strip into 16 – 1½" squares. Cut 8 squares into half-square triangles.

FROM THE LIGHT FABRIC, CUT:

1 – 2" x 4" strip. Cut the strip into 2 – 2" squares. Cut the squares into half-square triangles.

1 – 1½" x 9" strip. Cut the strip into 6 – 1½" squares. Cut the squares into half-square triangles.

1 – 1" x 12" strip. Cut the strip into 8 – 1" x 1½" rectangles.

FROM THE MEDIUM FABRIC, CUT:

1 – 1½" x 21" strip. Cut the strip into 14 – 1½" squares. Cut 6 squares into half-square triangles.

FROM THE DARK FABRIC, CUT:

1 – 1½" x 9" strip. Cut the strip into 6 – 1½" squares. Cut 2 squares into half-square triangles.

1 – 1" x 19" strip. Cut the strip into 8 – 1" x 1¾" rectangles and 4 – 1" x 1¼" rectangles.

ASSEMBLING THE BLOCK

Sew each Unit A to a Unit C as shown

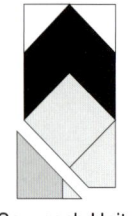

Sew each Unit D to Units E

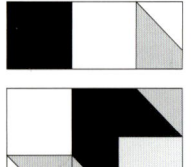

Sew each Unit B to Unit AC

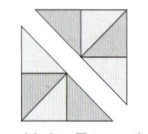

Sew Units F together

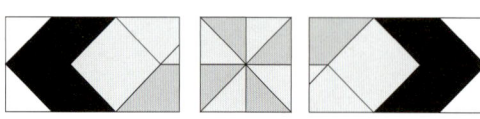

Sew Units DE to Units F

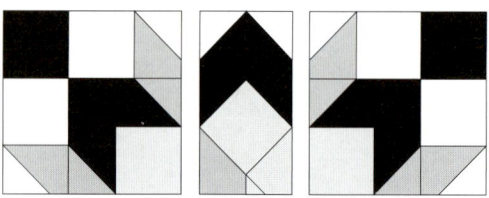

Sew Units ABC to Units DE

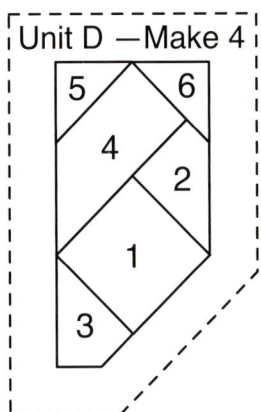
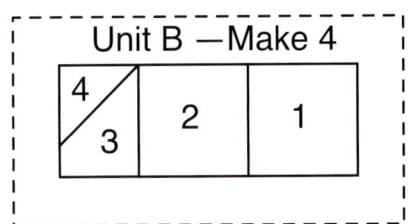
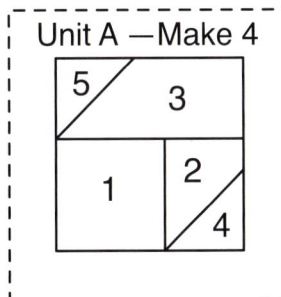
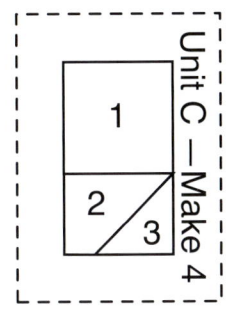
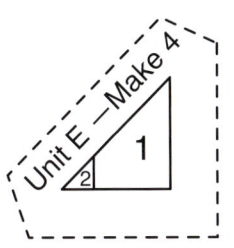
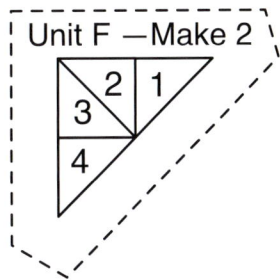

POSITION CHART

FABRIC	POSITION	SIZE	
Unit A–Make 4			
Medium	1	1½" x 1½"	
Dark	2	1" x 1¼"	
Dark	3	1" x 1¾"	
Light	4, 5	1½" x 1½"	◣
Unit B–Make 4			
Dark	1	1½" x 1½"	
Background	2	1½" x 1½"	
Light	3	1" x 1½"	
Background	4	1½" x 1½"	◣
Unit C–Make 4			
Background	1	1½" x 1½"	
Light	2	1" x 1½"	
Background	3	1½" x 1½"	◣
Unit D–Make 4			
Medium	1	1½" x 1½"	
Dark	2	1½" x 1½"	◣
Medium	3	1½" x 1½"	◣
Dark	4	1" x 1¾"	
Background	5, 6	1½" x 1½"	◣
Unit E–Make 4			
Light	1	2" x 2"	◣
Medium	2	1½" x 1½"	◣
Unit F–Make 2			
Light	1, 3	1½" x 1½"	◣
Medium	2, 4	1½" x 1½"	◣

Sew units together as shown

Chisholm Trail

MAY 1939 • 4" BLOCK

CUTTING INSTRUCTIONS

FROM THE BACKGROUND FABRIC, CUT:

1 – 2¾" square. Cut the square into half-square triangles.

1 – 2" x 10" strip. Cut the strip into 5 – 2" squares. Cut the squares into half-square triangles.

FROM THE MEDIUM FABRIC, CUT:

1 – 2" x 14" strip. Cut the strip into 7 – 2" squares. Cut the squares into half-square triangles.

FROM THE DARK FABRIC, CUT:

1 – 1¾" x 3½" strip. Cut the strip into 2 – 1¾" squares.

ASSEMBLING THE BLOCK

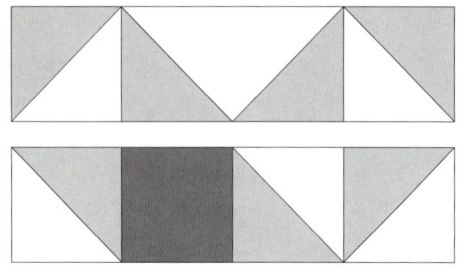

Sew each Unit A to each Unit B

Sew AB units together

100 | HARD TIMES, SPLENDID QUILTS

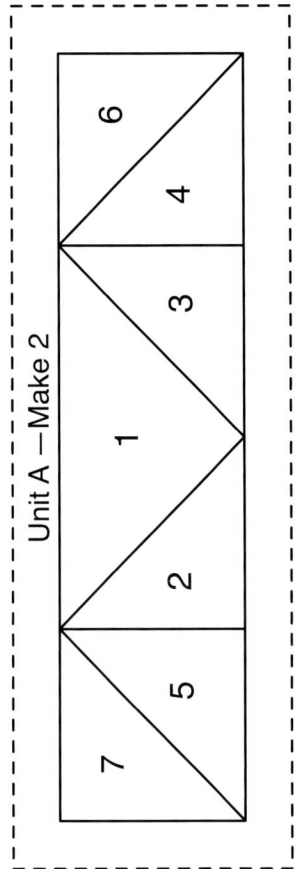
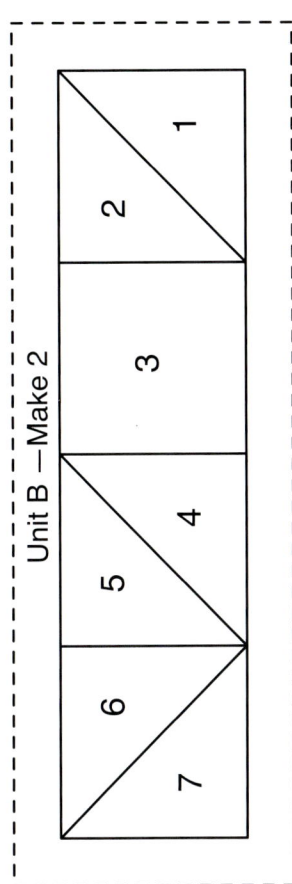

POSITION CHART

FABRIC	POSITION	SIZE	
Unit A–Make 2			
Background	1	2¾" x 2¾"	
Medium	2, 3, 6, 7	2" x 2"	
Background	4, 5	2" x 2"	
Unit B–Make 2			
Background	1, 5, 7	2" x 2"	
Medium	2, 4, 6	2" x 2"	
Dark	3	1¾" x 1¾"	

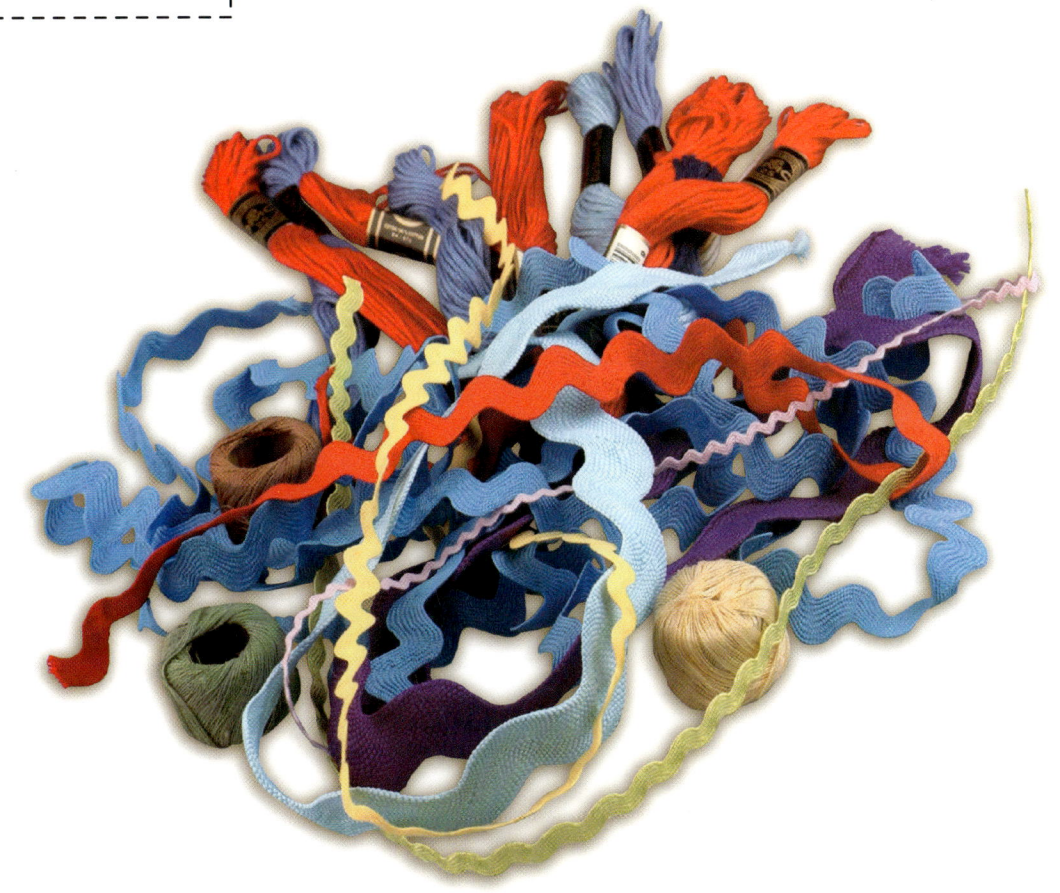

Wood Lily or Indian Head

MARCH 1936 • 4" BLOCK

CUTTING INSTRUCTIONS

FROM THE BACKGROUND FABRIC, CUT:

1 – 2¼" x 13½" strip. Cut the strip into 6 – 2¼" squares. Cut the squares into half-square triangles.

1 – 1¾" x 7" strip. Cut the strip into 4 – 1¾" squares. Cut the squares into half-square triangles.

FROM THE MEDIUM FABRIC, CUT:

1 – 1" x 28" strip. Cut the strip into 16 – 1" x 1¾" rectangles.

FROM THE DARK FABRIC, CUT:

1 – 2¼" x 4½" strip. Cut the strip into 2 – 2¼" squares. Cut the squares into half-square triangles.

1 – 1¼" x 7" strip. Cut the strip into 4 – 1¼" x 1¾" rectangles.

1 – 1" x 21" strip. Cut the strip into 12 – 1" x 1¾" rectangles.

ASSEMBLING THE BLOCK

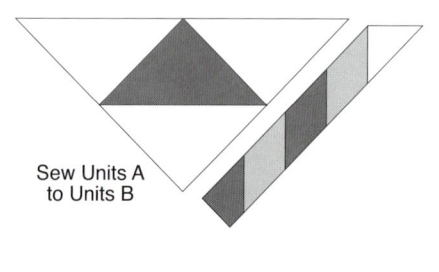

Sew Units A to Units B

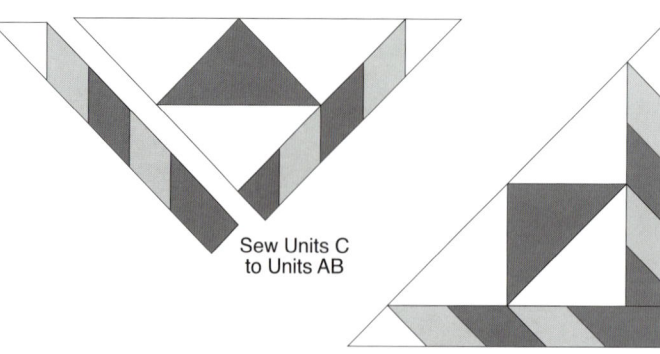

Sew Units C to Units AB

Sew Units ABC together

102 | HARD TIMES, SPLENDID QUILTS

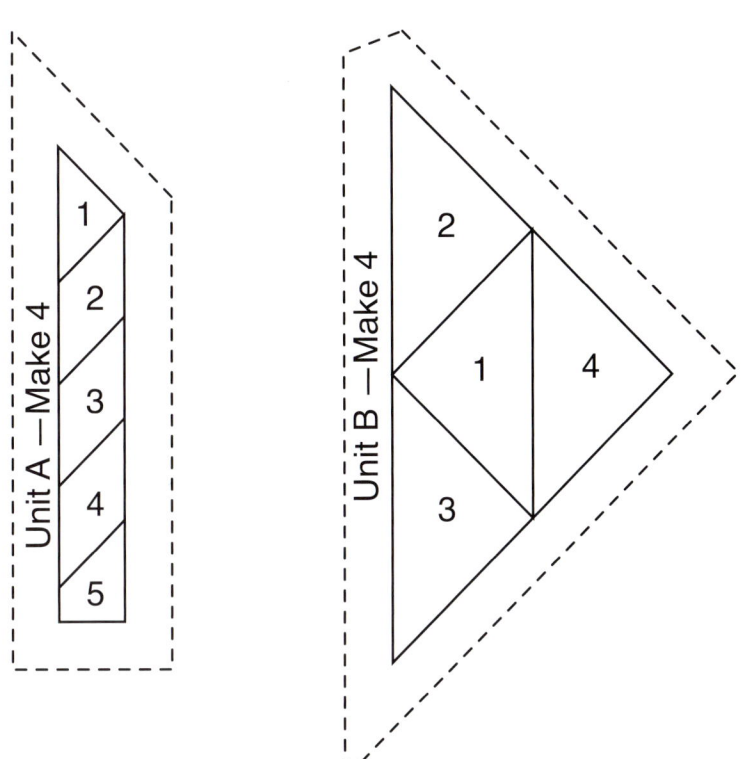

POSITION CHART

FABRIC	POSITION	SIZE	
Unit A–Make 4			
Background	1	1¾" x 1¾"	◣
Medium	2, 4	1" x 1¾"	
Dark	3, 5	1" x 1¾"	
Unit B–Make 4			
Dark	1	2¼" x 2¼"	◣
Background	2, 3, 4	2¼" x 2¼"	◣
Unit C–Make 4			
Background	1	1¾" x 1¾"	◣
Medium	2, 4	1" x 1¾"	
Dark	3	1" x 1¾"	
Dark	5	1¼" x 1¾"	

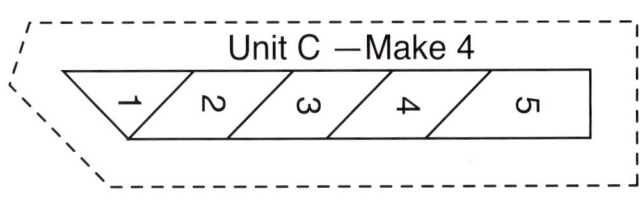

Complete the block as shown

4" WOOD LILY OR INDIAN HEAD | 103

Interlocked Squares

SEPTEMBER 1932 • 4" BLOCK

CUTTING INSTRUCTIONS

FROM THE BACKGROUND FABRIC, CUT:

1 – 2¾" x 5½" strip. Cut the strip into 2 – 2¾" squares. Cut the squares into half-square triangles.

1 – 1" x 22" strip. Cut the strip into 4 – 1" x 2½" rectangles and 4 – 1" x 3" rectangles.

FROM THE MEDIUM FABRIC, CUT:

1 – 2" x 4" strip. Cut the strip into 2 – 2" squares. Cut the squares into half-square triangles.

1 – 1¼" x 2½" strip. Cut the strip into 2 – 1¼" squares. Cut the squares into half-square triangles.

1 – 1" x 7" strip. Cut the strip into 4 – 1" x 1¾" rectangles.

FROM THE DARK FABRIC, CUT:

1 – 1¾" x 3½" strip. Cut the strip into 2 – 1¾" squares. Cut the squares into half-square triangles.

1 – 1" x 13" strip. Cut the strip into 4 – 1" x 3¼" rectangles.

ASSEMBLING THE BLOCK

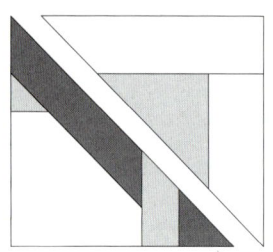

Sew Units A to Units B

Sew together as shown

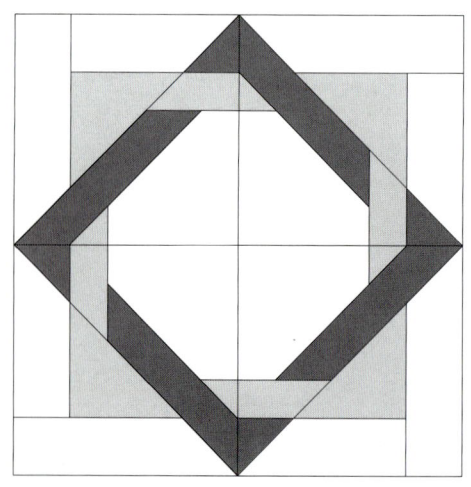

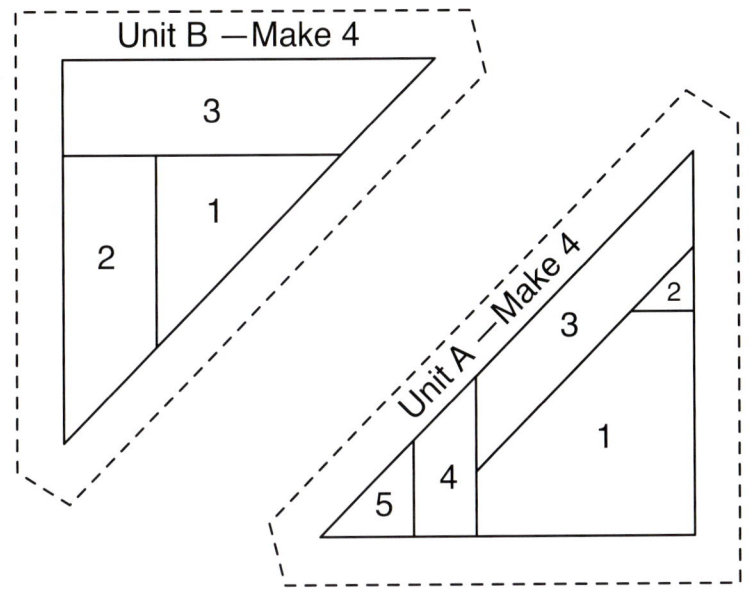

POSITION CHART

FABRIC	POSITION	SIZE	
Unit A-Make 4			
Background	1	2¾" x 2¾"	◣
Medium	2	1¼" x 1¼"	◣
Dark	3	1" x 3¼"	
Medium	4	1" x 1¾"	
Dark	5	1¾" x 1¾"	◣
Unit B-Make 4			
Medium	1	2" x 2"	◣
Background	2	1" x 2½"	
Background	3	1" x 3"	

Railroad Crossing

AUGUST 1935 • 4" BLOCK

CUTTING INSTRUCTIONS

FROM BACKGROUND FABRIC, CUT:

1 – 2¾" x 5½" strip. Cut into 2 – 2¾" squares. Cut the squares into half-square triangles.

1 – 1" x 9" strip. Cut the strip into 4 – 1" x 2¼" rectangles.

FROM MEDIUM FABRIC, CUT:

1 – 2¼" x 6¾" strip. Cut the strip into 3 – 2¼" squares. Cut 2 of the squares into half-square triangles.

1 – 1" x 18" strip. Cut the strip into 8 – 1" x 2¼" rectangles.

ASSEMBLING THE BLOCK

Sew Unit A to Unit B

Sew Units C to Unit AB

106 | HARD TIMES, SPLENDID QUILTS

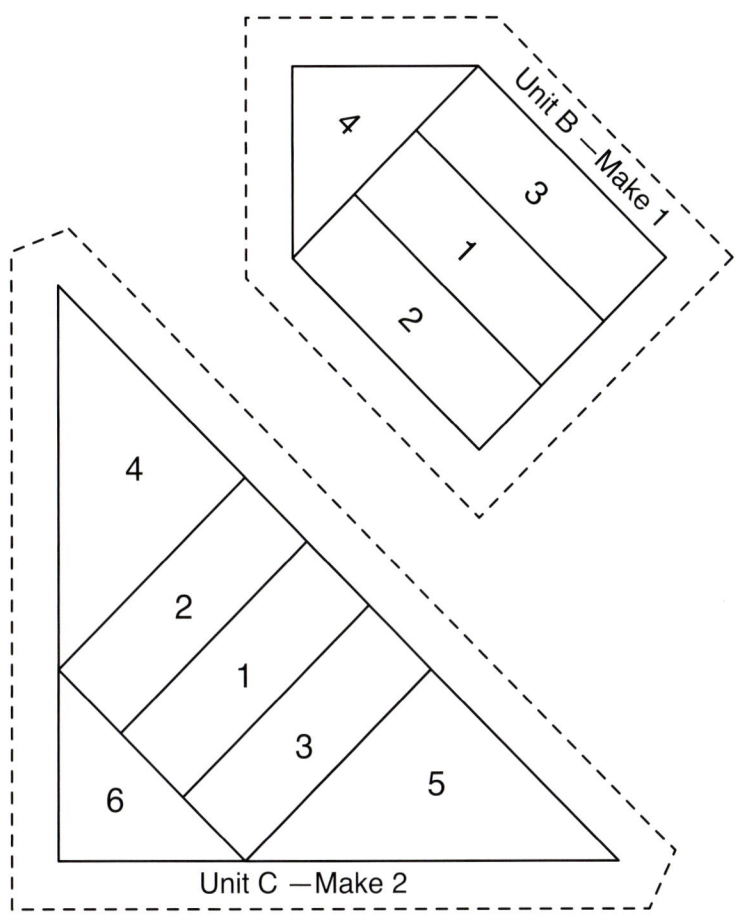

POSITION CHART

FABRIC	POSITION	SIZE	
Unit A-Make 1			
Background	1	1" x 2¼"	
Medium	2, 3	1" x 2¼"	
Medium	4	2¼" x 2¼"	◣
Medium	5	2¼" x 2¼"	
Unit B-Make 1			
Background	1	1" x 2¼"	
Medium	2, 3	1" x 2¼"	
Medium	4	2¼" x 2¼"	◣
Unit C-Make 2			
Background	1	1" x 2¼"	
Medium	2, 3	1" x 2¼"	
Background	4, 5	2¾" x 2¾"	◣
Medium	6	2¼" x 2¼"	◣

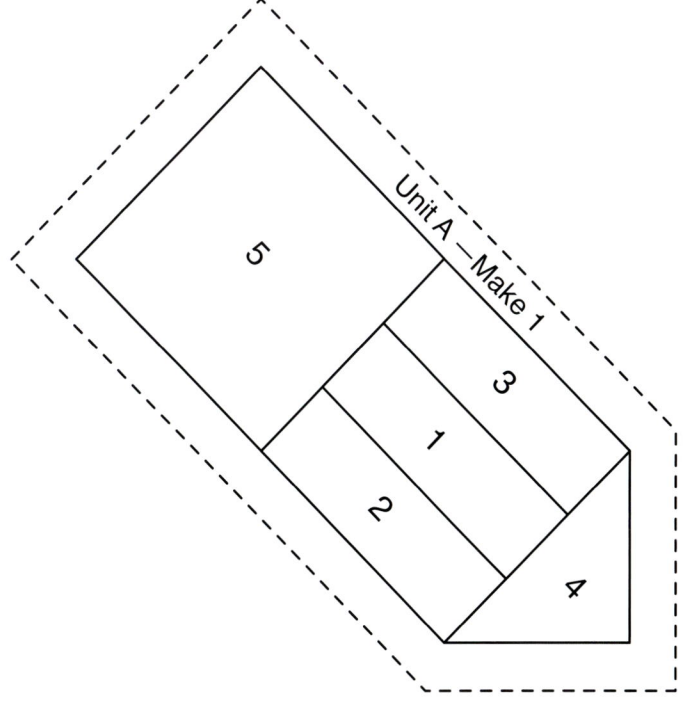

4" RAILROAD CROSSING | 107

The Basket

MAY 1938 • 4" BLOCK

CUTTING INSTRUCTIONS

FROM THE BACKGROUND FABRIC, CUT:

1 – 3½" square. Cut the square into half-square triangles. You will have one half-square triangle left over.

1 – 2¾" square. Cut the square into half-square triangles. You will have one half-square triangle left over.

1 – 2¼" x 4½" strip. Cut the strip into 2 – 2¼" squares. Cut the squares into half-square triangles. You will have one half-square triangle left over.

1 – 1¾" square. Cut the square into half-square triangles. You will have one half-square triangle left over.

1 – 1½" x 7" strip. Cut the strip into 2 – 1½" x 3½" rectangles.

1 – 1" x 9" strip. Cut the strip into 1 – 1" x 4¾" rectangle and 1 – 1" x 4¼" rectangle.

ASSEMBLING THE BLOCK

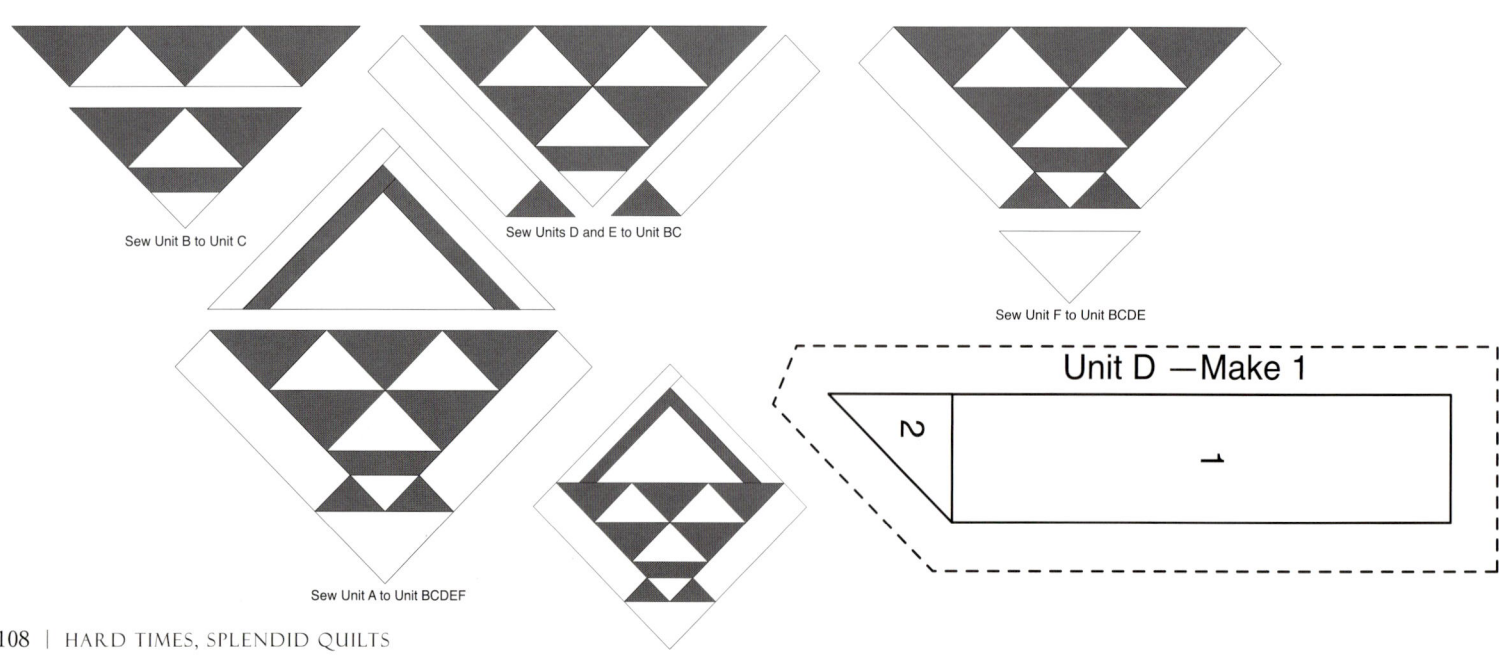

FROM THE MEDIUM FABRIC, CUT:

1 – 2¼" x 6¾" strip. Cut the strip into 3 – 2¼" squares. Cut the squares into half-square triangles. You will have one left over.

1 – 1¾" square. Cut the square into half-square triangles.

1 – ¾" x 9¾" strip. Cut the strip into 1 – ¾" x 2½" rectangle, 1 – ¾" x 3½" rectangle and 1 – ¾" x 3¾" rectangle.

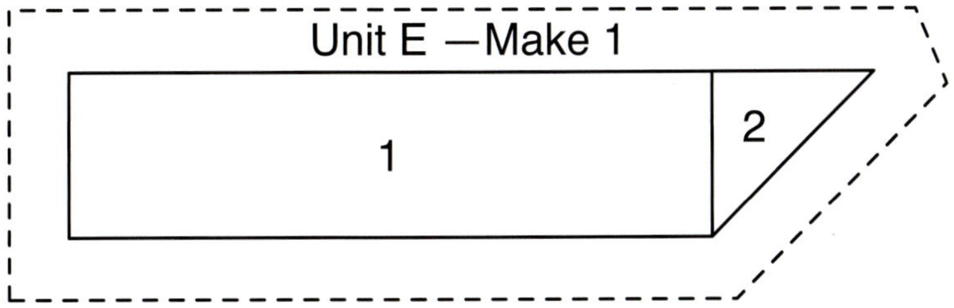

POSITION CHART

FABRIC	POSITION	SIZE	
Unit A-Make 1			
Background	1	3½" x 3½"	◣
Medium	2	¾" x 3½"	
Medium	3	¾" x 3¾"	
Background	4	1" x 4¼"	
Background	5	1" x 4¾"	
Unit B-Make 1			
Medium	1, 3, 5	2¼" x 2¼"	◣
Background	2, 4	2¼" x 2¼"	◣
Unit C-Make 1			
Medium	1, 5	2¼" x 2¼"	◣
Background	2	2¼" x 2¼"	◣
Medium	3	¾" x 2½"	
Background	4	1¾" x 1¾"	◣
Unit D-Make 1			
Background	1	1½" x 3½"	
Medium	2	1¾" x 1¾"	◣
Unit E-Make 1			
Background	1	1½" x 3½"	
Medium	2	1¾" x 1¾"	◣
Unit F-Make 1			
Background	1	2¾" x 2¾"	◣

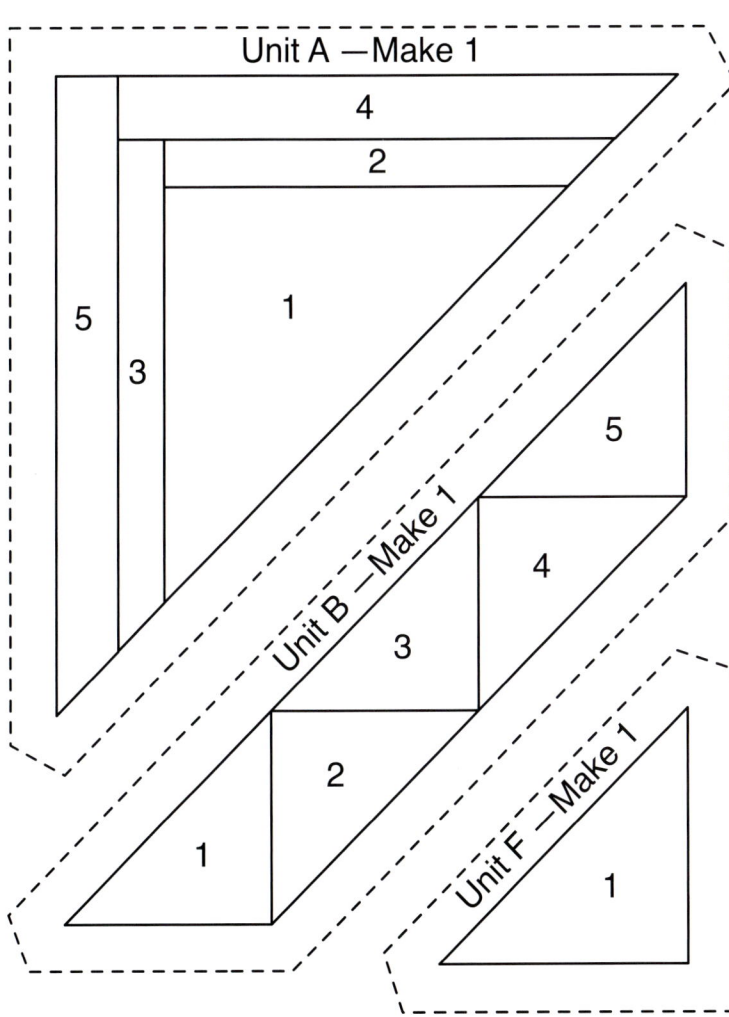

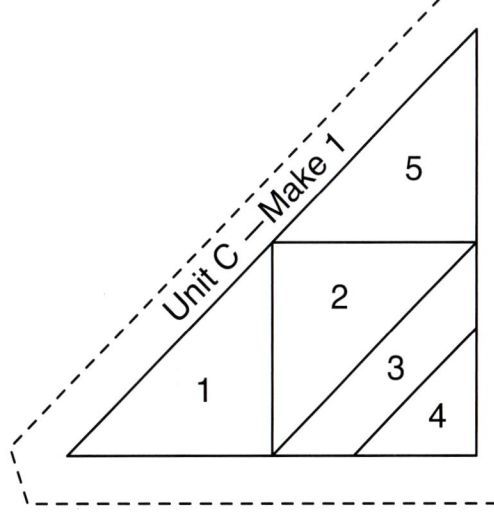

Grandmother's Favorite

NOVEMBER 1930 • 4" BLOCK

CUTTING INSTRUCTIONS

FROM THE BACKGROUND FABRIC, CUT:

1 – 3" square.

1 – 2" x 12" strip. Cut the strip into 6 – 2" squares. Cut the squares into half-square triangles.

1 – 1¾" x 3½" strip. Cut the strip into 2 – 1¾" squares. Cut the squares into half-square triangles.

FROM THE MEDIUM FABRIC, CUT:

1 – 2" x 4" strip. Cut into 2 – 2" squares. Cut the squares into half-square triangles.

1 – 1¾" x 10½" strip. Cut into 6 – 1¾" squares. Cut the squares into half-square triangles.

ASSEMBLING THE BLOCK

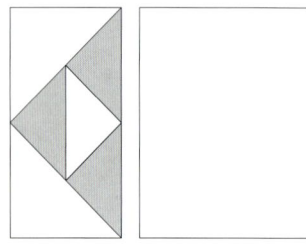

Sew Unit B to Unit C

Sew each Unit A to Unit BC

110 | HARD TIMES, SPLENDID QUILTS

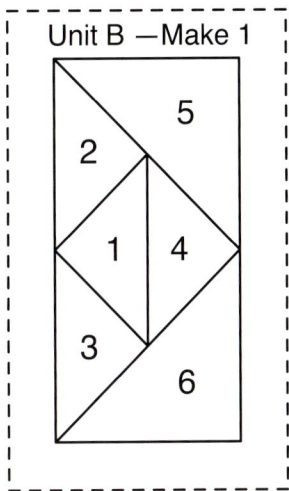

POSITION CHART

FABRIC	POSITION	SIZE	
Unit A–Make 2			
Background	1	1¾" x 1¾"	◣
Medium	2, 3, 4	1¾" x 1¾"	◣
Background	5, 6, 9, 10	2" x 2"	◣
Medium	7, 8	2" x 2"	◣
Unit B–Make 1			
Background	1	1¾" x 1¾"	◣
Medium	2, 3, 4	1¾" x 1¾"	◣
Background	5, 6	2" x 2"	◣
Unit C–Make 1			
Background	1	1¾" x 1¾"	◣
Medium	2, 3, 4	1¾" x 1¾"	◣
Background	5, 6	2" x 2"	◣
Background	7	3" x 3"	◣

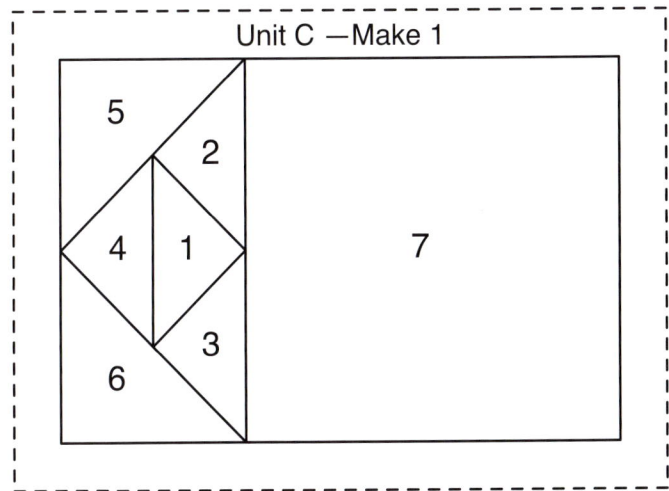

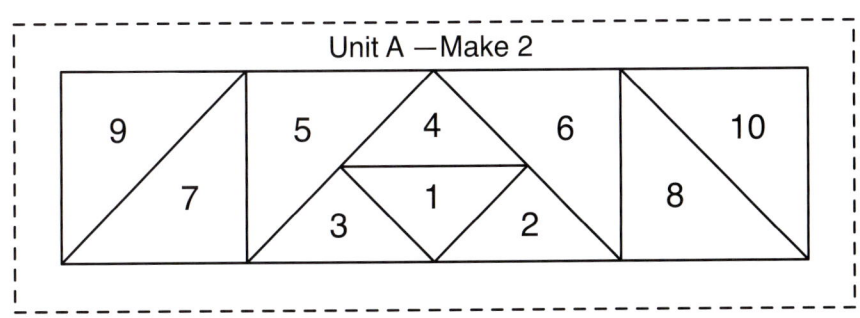

4" GRANDMOTHER'S FAVORITE

The Kaleidoscope

AUGUST 1930 • 4" BLOCK

CUTTING INSTRUCTIONS

FROM THE BACKGROUND FABRIC, CUT:

1 – 2¼" x 9" strip. Cut the strip into 4 – 2¼" squares.

1 – 2" x 4" strip. Cut the strip into 2 – 2" squares. Cut the squares into half-square triangles.

1 – 1½" x 15" strip. Cut the strip into 10 – 1½" squares. Cut the squares into half-square triangles.

FROM THE MEDIUM FABRIC, CUT:

1 – 2¼" square.

1 – 1½" x 18" strip. Cut the strip into 12 – 1½" squares. Cut the squares into half-square triangles.

FROM THE DARK FABRIC, CUT:

1 – 1½" x 3" strip. Cut the strip into 2 – 1½" squares. Cut the squares into half-square triangles.

ASSEMBLING THE BLOCK

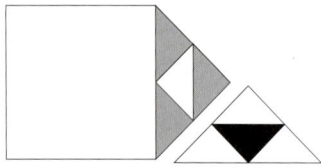
Sew Units B to Units C

Sew Units A to Units BC

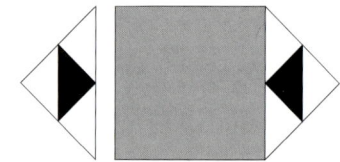
Sew Unit C to Unit F

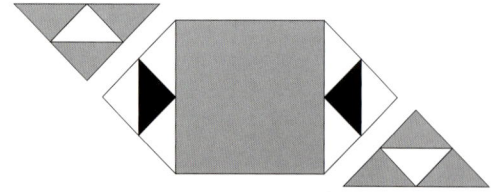
Sew Units E to Unit CF

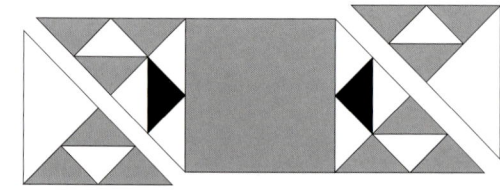
Sew Units D to Unit CEF

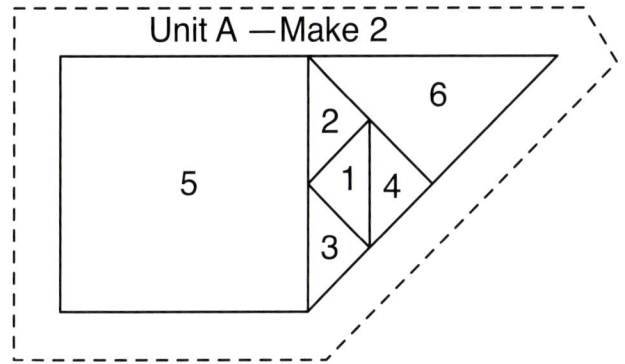

POSITION CHART

FABRIC	POSITION	SIZE
Unit A-Make 2		
Background	1	1½" x 1½"
Medium	2, 3, 4	1½" x 1½"
Background	5	2¼" x 2¼"
Background	6	2" x 2"
Unit B-Make 2		
Background	1	1½" x 1½"
Medium	2, 3, 4	1½" x 1½"
Background	5	2¼" x 2¼"
Unit C-Make 3		
Dark	1	1½" x 1½"
Background	2, 3, 4	1½" x 1½"
Unit D-Make 2		
Background	1	1½" x 1½"
Medium	2, 3, 4	1½" x 1½"
Background	5	2" x 2"
Unit E-Make 2		
Background	1	1½" x 1½"
Medium	2, 3, 4	1½" x 1½"
Unit F-Make 1		
Dark	1	1½" x 1½"
Background	2, 3, 4	1½" x 1½"
Medium	5	2¼" x 2¼"

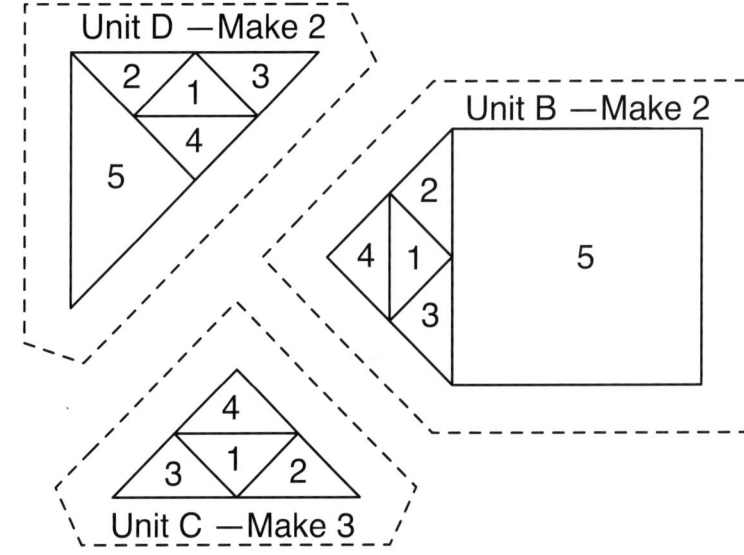

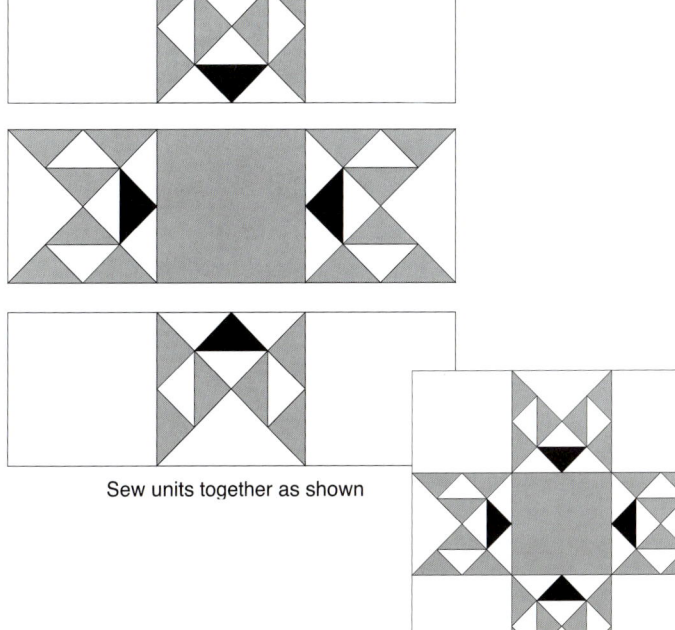

Sew units together as shown

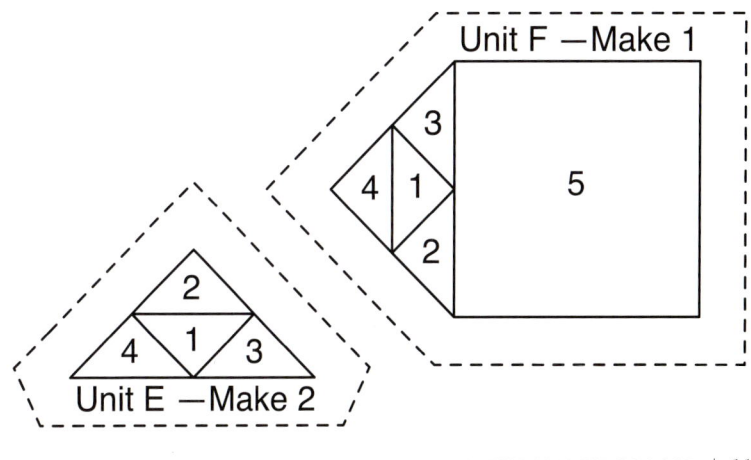

4" THE KALEIDOSCOPE | 113

Jackson Star

MAY 1931 • 4" BLOCK

CUTTING INSTRUCTIONS

FROM THE BACKGROUND FABRIC, CUT:

1 – 2" square.

1 – 1¾" x 24½" strip. Cut the strip into 14 – 1¾" squares. Cut the squares into half-square triangles.

1 – 1¼" x 5" strip. Cut the strip into 4 – 1¼" squares.

FROM THE MEDIUM FABRIC, CUT:

1 – 1½" x 8" strip. Cut the strip into 4 – 1½" x 2" rectangles.

1 – 1" x 6" strip. Cut the strip into 4 – 1" x 1½" rectangles.

FROM THE DARK FABRIC, CUT:

1 – 1¾" x 7" strip. Cut the strip into 4 – 1¾" squares. Cut into half-square triangles.

1 – 1" x 26" strip. Cut the strip into 8 – 1" x 1¾" rectangles and 4 – 1" x 3" rectangles.

ASSEMBLING THE BLOCK

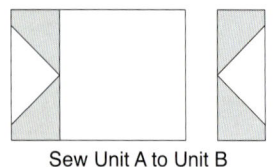

Sew Unit A to Unit B

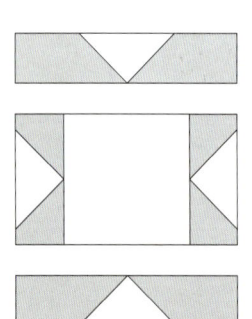

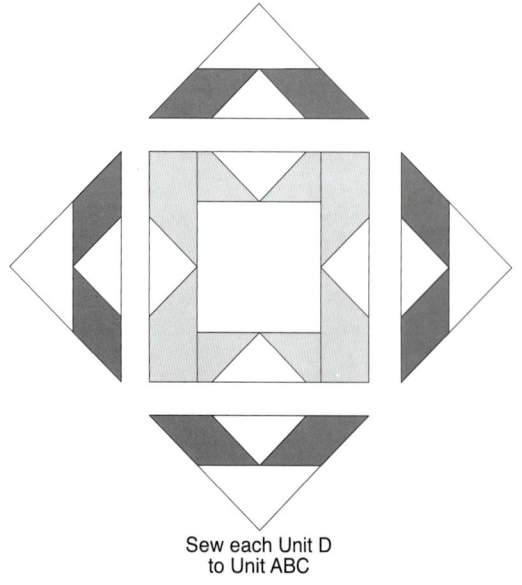

Sew each Unit D to Unit ABC

Sew each Unit E to ABCD

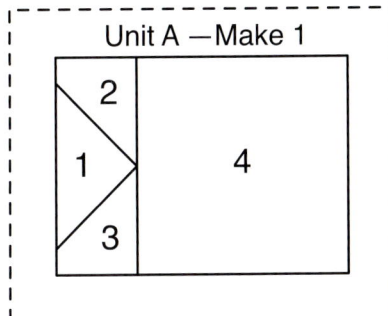
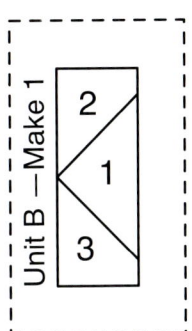
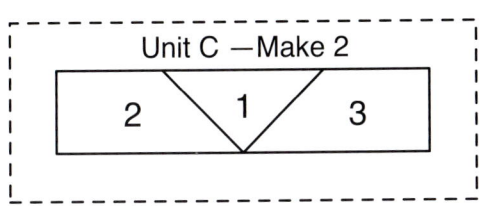
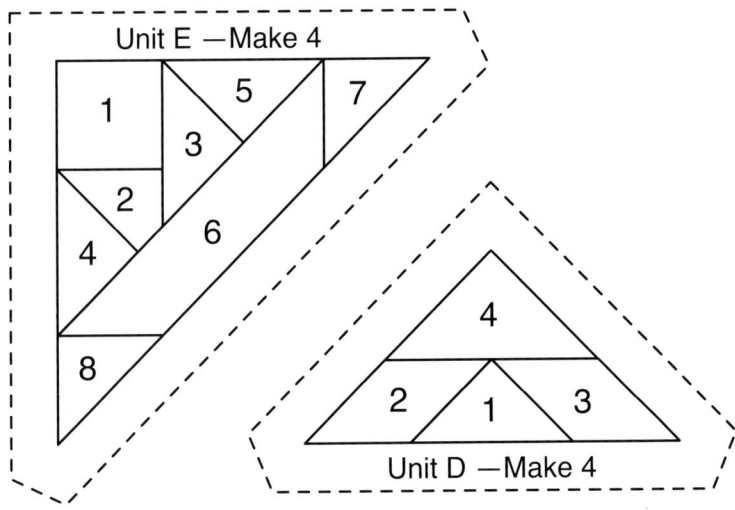

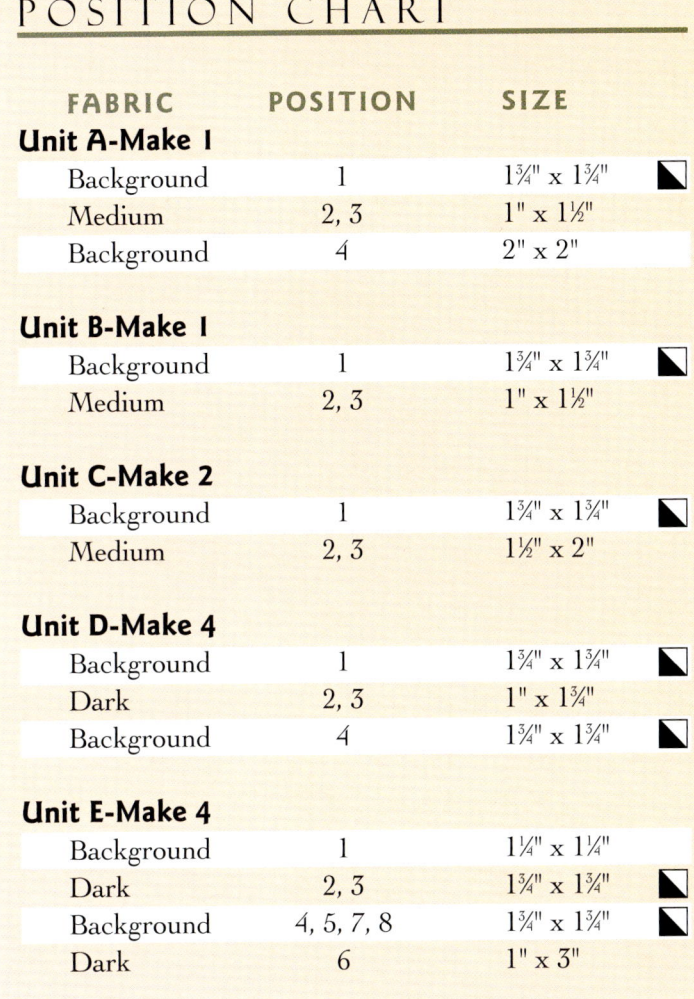

POSITION CHART

FABRIC	POSITION	SIZE	
Unit A–Make 1			
Background	1	1¾" x 1¾"	◣
Medium	2, 3	1" x 1½"	
Background	4	2" x 2"	
Unit B–Make 1			
Background	1	1¾" x 1¾"	◣
Medium	2, 3	1" x 1½"	
Unit C–Make 2			
Background	1	1¾" x 1¾"	◣
Medium	2, 3	1½" x 2"	
Unit D–Make 4			
Background	1	1¾" x 1¾"	◣
Dark	2, 3	1" x 1¾"	
Background	4	1¾" x 1¾"	◣
Unit E–Make 4			
Background	1	1¼" x 1¼"	
Dark	2, 3	1¾" x 1¾"	◣
Background	4, 5, 7, 8	1¾" x 1¾"	◣
Dark	6	1" x 3"	

4" JACKSON STAR | 115

The Christmas Tree

DECEMBER 1932 • 4" BLOCK

CUTTING INSTRUCTIONS

FROM THE BACKGROUND FABRIC, CUT:

1 – 3" x 10" strip. Cut the strip into 2 – 3" x 5" rectangles.

1 – 1½" x 4½" strip. Cut the strip into 2 – 1½" x 2¼" rectangles.

1 – 1¼" x 6" strip. Cut the strip into 4 – 1¼" x 1½" rectangles.

1 – 1" x 30" strip. Cut the strip into 20 – 1" x 1½" rectangles.

FROM THE MEDIUM FABRIC, CUT:

1 – 1½" square.

1 – 1" x 4½" strip. Cut the strip into 3 – 1" x 1½" rectangles.

1 – ¾" x 30" strip. Cut the strip into 20 – ¾" x 1½" rectangles.

ASSEMBLING THE BLOCK

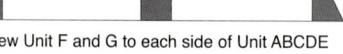

116 | HARD TIMES, SPLENDID QUILTS

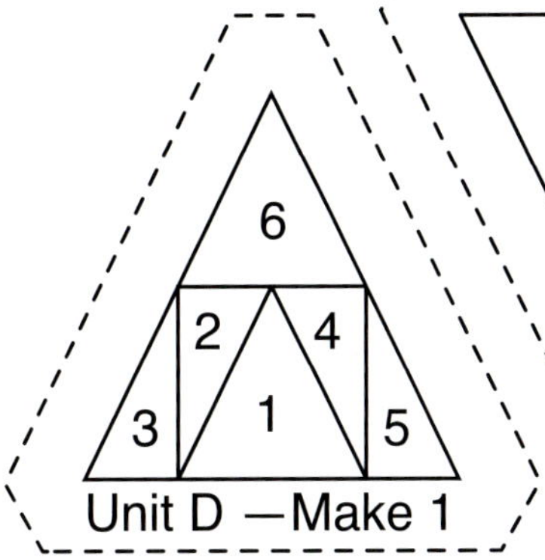

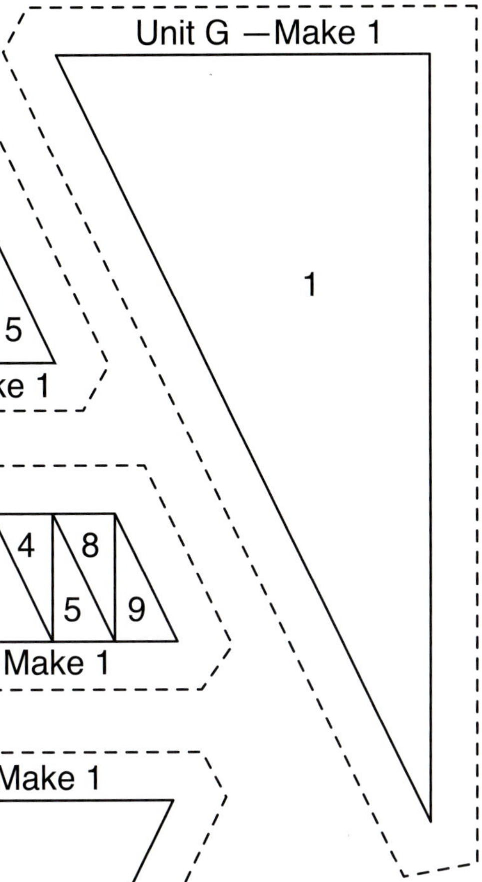

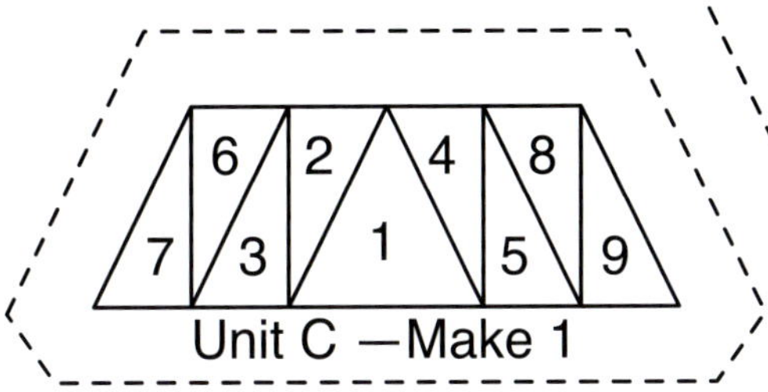

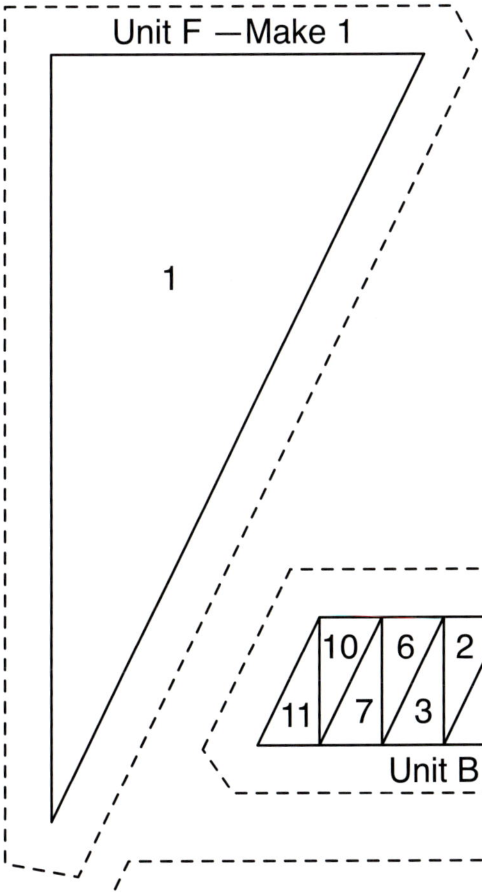

POSITION CHART

FABRIC	POSITION	SIZE
Unit A–Make 1		
Background	1	1¼" x 1½"
Medium	2, 4, 6, 8, 10, 12, 14, 16	¾" x 1½"
Background	3, 5, 7, 9, 11, 13, 15, 17	1" x 1½"
Unit B–Make 1		
Background	1	1¼" x 1½"
Medium	2, 4, 6, 8, 10, 12	¾" x 1½"
Background	3, 5, 7, 9, 11, 13	1" x 1½"
Unit C–Make 1		
Background	1	1¼" x 1½"
Medium	2, 4, 6, 8	¾" x 1½"
Background	3, 5, 7, 9	1" x 1½"
Unit D–Make 1		
Background	1	1¼" x 1½"
Medium	2, 4	¾" x 1½"
Background	3, 5	1" x 1½"
Medium	6	1½" x 1½"
Unit E–Make 1		
Medium	1	1" x 1½"
Background	2, 3	1½" x 2¼"
Medium	4, 5	1" x 1½"
Units F & G–Make 1 each		
Background	1	3" x 5"

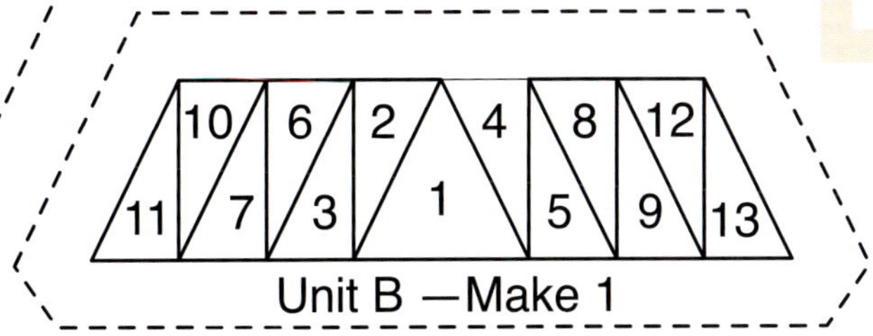

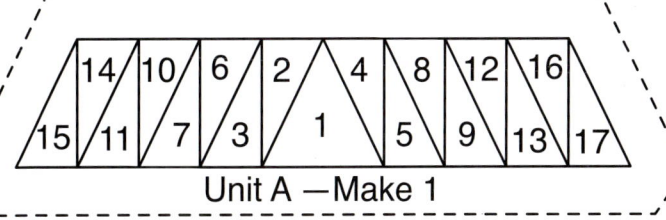

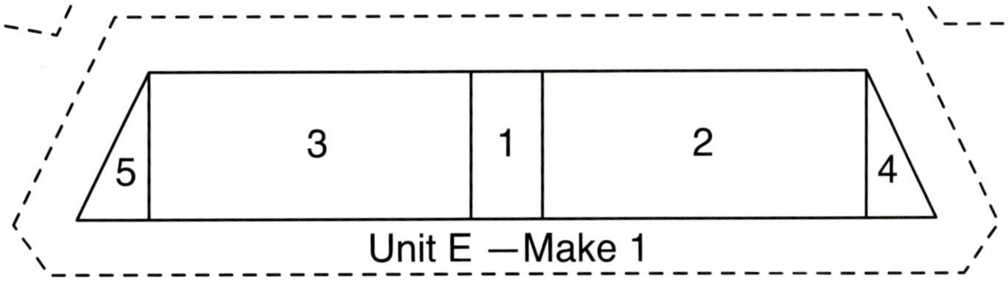

4" THE CHRISTMAS TREE

Miniature Quilt

FINISHING INSTRUCTIONS
TO MAKE THE QUILT

After making 20 blocks, choose 4 blocks that will be the corners of your border. Set aside to be used later. The Christmas Tree does not work well on point.

Sashing: Cut 10 – 1¼" strips across the width of the fabric. Cut into 32 – 1¼" x 4½" rectangles and 32 – 1¼" x 6" rectangles.

Sew a 1¼" x 4½" strip on the top and bottom of 16 blocks. Sew the 1¼" x 6" rectangles on both sides.

Solid blocks: Cut 2 – 6" strips across the width of the fabric. Cut the strips into 6" squares. You will need 9 squares.

Setting triangles: Cut 1 – 9" strip across the width of the fabric. Cut 3 – 9" squares from the strip. Cut each square on the diagonal from corner to corner twice. Each square will yield 4 pieces. You will need 12 setting triangles.

Setting corner triangles: Cut 2 – 4¾" squares. Cut the squares on the diagonal from corner to corner. Each square will yield 2 triangles. You will need 4 triangles.

Sew the quilt blocks together using the solid blocks, setting triangles and setting corner triangles.

For the first border, cut 4 – 1¼" strips the width of the fabric. Measure the width of the quilt and cut the length needed, sew onto both sides. Press. Measure the top and bottom, cut the length needed. Sew on the top and bottom of the quilt.

For the second border, cut 4 – 4½" strips the width of the fabric. Measure the width of the quilt and cut the 4 lengths needed, sew on both sides. Press. Sew a block on both ends of the top and bottom border. Sew the borders onto the quilt.

Layer the quilt with batting and backing. Quilt. For binding, cut 4 – 2½" strips the width of the fabric.

Photo Album

These photo albums were made by Carolyn Cullinan McCormick, Franktown, Colorado.

PHOTO ALBUM SUPPLY LIST
- 12" x 12" Linen Cloth Photo Album
- 3 – 2 ounce Acrylic Paints (Dark, Medium, Light)
- 2 – 1" Foam Brushes
- Blue Removable Painter's Tape
- Newspaper to Protect Table
- Plastic Wrap
- Rubber Gloves (Optional—the paint will come off hands with soap and water.)
- ¼ yard Light Fabric
- ¼ yard Medium Fabric
- Fabric Sheet for Picture (Optional)
- 12" square Backing
- 12" square Batting
- ⅛ yard Binding
- 1¼ yard Trim
- Tacky Glue

INSTRUCTIONS

Remove the inside pages. If the album comes apart, separate the front from the back. Use blue painter's tape and tape along the inside of the album where the fabric ends and the paper starts. Also tape a piece of plastic wrap on the inside of the front and back of the album to protect it.

Lay out the newspaper to protect the table. If you are placing a quilt block on the front of the album, you only need to paint in about 2" from the edges. Use one foam brush to apply the dark acrylic paint. Before it dries, dip the other brush into the medium and the light colors at the same time and apply randomly. Keep painting until you get the effect you want. Let the paint dry, then remove the tape.

Make the quilt block of your choice for the front of the album. Add a picture into the quilt block if you desire.

Quilt and bind.

Glue the block on the album with tacky glue.

Add the trim using tacky glue.

Give to a good friend.

Feathered Edge Star Quilt

SIX 10" BLOCKS

FEATHERED EDGE STAR QUILT SUPPLY LIST
Fabric requirements:
- **Background:**
  Blocks: 1 ¼ yards
- **Medium:**
  Blocks: 1 yard
  Blank blocks and setting triangles: 1¼ yard
  Second border: 3/4 yard
  Total: 3 yards
- **Dark:**
  Blocks: ⅜ yard
  Sashing: ⅜ yard
  First Border: ¼ yard
  Binding: ½ yard
  Total: 1½ yards

Backing: 2¾ yard
Batting: 1⅜ yard of 90 wide

Feathered Star made by Carolyn Cullinan McCormick, Franktown, Colorado, quilted by Tracy Peterson Yadon, Lady Quilter, Manhattan, Montana.

INSTRUCTIONS

FROM THE BACKGROUND FABRIC, CUT:

Cut 4 – 4¼" strips across the width of the fabric. Cut the strips into 30 – 4¼" squares. Cut 6 of the squares into half-square triangles.

Cut 1– 3" strip across the width of the fabric. Cut the strip into 12– 3" squares.

Cut 10 – 2" strips the width of the fabric. Cut the strips into 180 – 2" squares. Cut the squares into half-square triangles.

FROM THE MEDIUM FABRIC, CUT:

Cut 2 – 3¼" strips the width of the fabric. Cut the strips into 12 – 3¼" squares. Cut the squares into half-square triangles.

Cut 7 – 2" strips the width of the fabric. Cut the strips into 120 – 2" squares. Cut the squares into half-square triangles.

Cut 5 – 1½" strips across the width of the fabric. Cut the strips into 48 – 1½" x 2¼" rectangles and 48 – 1½" squares.

FROM THE DARK FABRIC, CUT:

Cut 3 – 3¼" strips across the width of the fabric. Cut the strips into 30 – 3¼" squares. Cut 24 of the squares into half-square triangles.

Follow the position chart for the Feathered Edge Star on pages 24 and 25.

SASHING:

Cut 8 – 1½" strips across the width of the fabric. Cut the strips into 12 – 1½" x 10½" rectangles and 12 – 1½" x 12½" rectangles.

Sew a 1½" x 10½" rectangle on the top and bottom of each block. Sew the 1½" x 12½" rectangle on both sides.

SOLID BLOCKS:

Cut 1 – 12½" strip across the width of the fabric. Cut into 2 – 12½" squares.

SETTING TRIANGLES:

Cut 1 – 18¼" strip across the width of the fabric. From the strip, cut 2 – 18¼" squares. Cut on the diagonal from corner to corner twice. Each square will yield 4 pieces. You will need 6 setting triangles.

SETTING CORNER TRIANGLES:

Cut 2 – 9⅜" squares. Cut the squares on the diagonal from corner to corner. Each square will yield 2 triangles. You will need 4 triangles.

Sew the quilt blocks together using the solid blocks, setting triangles and setting corner triangles.

For the first border, cut 5 – 1½" strips across the width of the fabric. Measure the width of the quilt at the top and bottom, then measure and cut the strips the width of the quilt. Sew on the top and bottom. Press. Measure the length of the quilt, then measure and cut strips the length of the quilt. You will have to join two strips together. Sew on both sides. Press.

For the second border, cut 5 – 4" strips across the width of the fabric. Follow the same procedure as above.

Layer the quilt top together with the batting and backing and quilt.

Cut 6 – 2½" strips the width of the fabric for binding. Sew together. Press in half.

Shadow Box

SHADOW BOX SUPPLY LIST
- 11" x 14" shadow box
- Scrap fabric and batting for quilt block
- Miscellaneous sewing supplies
- Self-sticking Velcro or glue gun

INSTRUCTIONS

Make a 4" quilt block using scrap fabric. Layer the block, backing and batting and quilt.

Lay the shadow box flat and remove the back. Position the items on the back and the ledge of the box.

Play and have fun with the articles you have chosen to put in the box. When you are happy with the arrangement, fasten everything into place. Let the glue dry and replace the back of the box.

This shadow box, made by Carolyn Cullinan McCormick, Franktown, Colorado, is a wonderful way to show off prized possessions.